Letts explore

The Merchant of Venice

William Shakespeare

Guide written by John Mahoney

A Letts Literature Guide for GCSE

Contents

The Merchant of Venice

ANTONIO IS VERY MELANCHOLY

BASSANIO ASKS ANTONIO FOR A LOAN TO TRY TO WIN **PORTIA'S** HAND IN MARRIAGE.

ANTONIO WILL BORRO THE MONEY TO LEND TO HIS GOO FRIEND AS HIS CREDIT IS GOOD.

I MAY NEITHER CHOOSE WHO I WOULD, NOR REFUSE WHO I DISLIKE

NERISSA AND PORTIA REMEMBER **BASSANIO** AS BEING WORTHY OF PRAISE.

BACK IN VENICE, **ANTONIO** AND **BASSANIO** ASK **SHYLOCK** FOR A LOAN OF **3000 DUCATS**.

YOU CALL ME MISBELIEVER

AN EQUAL POUND OF YOUR FAIR FLESH.

BACK IN BELMONT, **THE PRINCE OF MOROCCO** ARRIVES

YOU MUST TAKE YOUR CHANCE

LAUNCELOT ASKS TO BECOME BASSANIO'S SERVANT.

BASSANIO INVITES GRATIANO TO GO WITH HIM TO BELMONT.

OUR HOUSE IS HELL!

LORENZO, GRATIANO AND SOLANIO ARE PREPARING FOR BASSANIO'S MASQUE.

LORENZO TELLS GRATIANO OF JESSICA'S PLAN TO ROB SHYLOCK.

JESSICA IS IN CHARGE OF THE HOUSE WHILE SHYLOCK GOES TO THE MASQUE.

LORENZO AND HIS FRIENDS RESCUE JESSICA, DISGUISED AS A PAGE BOY.

THE **PRINCE OF MOROCCO** CHOOSES THE GOLD CASKET.

All that glisters is not gold...

MOROCCO LEAVES...

SOLANIO AND **SALERIO** GOSSIP.

THE **PRINCE OF ARRAGON** CHOOSES THE SILVER CASKET.

A fool's head

PORTIA HEARS THAT **BASSANIO** WILL SHORTLY BE ARRIVING TO TRY HIS LUCK. **SHE** AND **NERISSA** ARE HOPEFUL.

LET HIM LOOK TO HIS BOND

IF YOU PRICK US, DO WE NOT BLEED?

I WOULD MY DAUGHTER WERE DEAD AT MY FEET!

BASSANIO CHOOSES THE LEAD CASKET AND WINS **PORTIA**.

BUT WHEN THIS RING PARTS FROM THIS FINGER, THEN PARTS LIFE FROM HENCE.

NEWS ARRIVES OF **ANTONIO'S** PLIGHT, AND **BASSANIO** AND **GRATIANO** DECIDE TO FLEE.

PORTIA AND **NERISSA** HAVE A PLAN.

HOW SHALT THOU HOPE FOR MERCY, RENDERING NONE?

THE QUALITY OF MERCY IS NOT STRAIN'D

ANTONIO ALLOWS **SHYLOCK** TO LIVE ON TWO CONDITIONS.

BASSANIO IS FORCED TO GIVE UP HIS RING.

BACK IN BELMONT, THE THREE LOVING COUPLES ARE HAPPY AT LAST.

Who's who in *The Merchant of Venice*

Antonio

Antonio is the Merchant of Venice of the play's title. His opening speech, which begins 'In sooth I know not why I am so sad. It wearies me', sets the scene for the events that will befall him during most of the play. Why is he sad? Is it a device used by Shakespeare to set the initial mood of the play? Melancholy was a fashionable affectation in Elizabethan times and Shakespeare may well be attributing this to the rich Venetians: note how the rich heiress, Portia, also declares that she is weary. Most likely Antonio is sad because he knows that the close relationship he has with Bassanio is about to be upset by the latter's wish to seek Portia's hand in marriage. Though it is almost certainly not intended as a homosexual relationship, Antonio makes extravagant (and well-supported) claims for what he would do for Bassanio, and his isolation at the end of the play derives largely from Bassanio's marriage.

Antonio stands for love and friendship in contrast to Shylock's calculating greed. In agreeing to finance Bassanio's pursuit of Portia he provides for the disruption of his own deep relationship with his friend. He is quite prepared to use his good name to seek money for Bassanio, and then to agree to a forfeit that puts his life in jeopardy.

Antonio is melancholy, passive in his acceptance of events, somewhat unemotional in response to the threat to his life and is ultimately a lonely figure at the end of the play. If we are to see Antonio as an ideal of selfless generosity, as Shakespeare sometimes appears to suggest, his attitude to Jews is a problem. His contempt for usury and insistence on Shylock's conversion can be explained away as normal, even Christian, for the time, but not his constant insults and the fact that he spits on Shylock.

Bassanio

When we meet Bassanio he is in debt and wants to borrow money to pursue Portia in order 'to get clear of all the debts I owe'. He gives no security to his friend, and when he gets the money he spends it on liveries for his servants and a party: not an auspicious start. He is a spendthrift who is unconcerned about borrowing money from a friend in order to finance his adventures. When departing for Belmont, he agrees to take his friend Gratiano along, despite believing him to be rude and wild: clearly not an ideal person to participate in such a delicate mission. This is either a very generous or very foolhardy gesture on Bassanio's part.

However, he must have good points. Antonio is certainly prepared to trust him. Bassanio does show some sensitivity to the matter of asking for yet more money: his archery image (Act 1, Scene 1) suggests he feels he ought to justify his request. And he warns Antonio against the bond, so he shows some sense, though he still accepts the money!

Nerissa calls Bassanio 'a scholar and a soldier'. His choice of the correct casket, lead, indicates that he is also of a thinker, not easily taken in by appearances. There seems no doubt that he genuinely loves Portia and he is honest about his debt to Antonio. On hearing of the latter's trouble he goes immediately to provide assistance and shows his concern throughout the trial. He is seen to be a very different man at the end of the play to the one we met at the beginning. Like many young men in Shakespearean comedy, Bassanio has matured through the tests that he has faced. In finally passing those tests and accepting his errors, he is able to enter into an equal partnership with Portia rather than having to rely on on an indulgent older friend.

Shylock

Shylock demonstrates the stock features of the Elizabethan caricature of a Jew: hatred of Christians and the practice of usury (lending money that must be repaid with interest). This latter is something which our society virtually lives by, but the Elizabethans had rather different views. Although Shylock's name has become equated with the warped greed of the miser, few who read the play can help feeling some degree of sympathy with his misfortunes.

Almost more than any other Shakespearean character, the way in which Shylock has been viewed has changed through the centuries. In the eighteenth century he was considered an out-and-out villain whose 'savage fierceness and fellness … cannot agree either with the style or characters of comedy'. In the nineteenth century it became common to concentrate on the wrongs suffered by Shylock, to the extent that at one time it was fashionable to finish the play at the end of the trial scene, and the great Henry Irving portrayed him as 'a heroic saint'. The varied interpretations in the modern theatre are, at least, less extreme than these.

The problem is that Shakespeare begins with the stock caricature of the Jew — resemblances to Marlowe's earlier Jew of Malta are clear. However, Shakespeare's character then develops a more genuine human dimension, in the same way as his Christians fall far short of perfection. The result is a character who indeed suffers wrongs, who has a valid point of view on Christian failings, but is in no way to be seen as admirable. Nor, unlike Barabas in *The Jew of Malta*, is he the central character of the play, though certainly the most challenging male role.

Essentially, audience sympathy is turned away from Shylock by his hatred of Antonio (to the extent of murder) and his ruthless pursuit of profit. His eloquent description of Antonio's abusive language and behaviour redresses the balance a little in his favour. Equally, his daughter's elopement with a Christian and the theft of his money and jewels gives us pause for thought about our attitude towards him. However, the comic way in which he is presented as reacting to the theft, and his cry of 'my ducats', evokes laughter not sympathy. He also mentions his ducats before his daughter, giving the impression that the money is the greater loss.

Shylock's famous speech 'If you prick us' (Act 3, Scene 1) again makes us reconsider our attitudes towards him, but then he spoils his plea by using it to justify plain revenge. The trial scene shows Shylock at his worst. He comes prepared with his own scales to weigh the flesh, and with a knife which he keeps sharpening, determined to cut the flesh himself. He rejects any plea for justice to be tempered by mercy. His observation when asked about a surgeon — that the bond did not require it — is cruel. When justice is eventually served and Shylock gets the sharp end, he has lost the audience's sympathy. Even Portia's failure to be merciful to him does not upset us unduly.

Portia

Portia is seen from the outset as someone above the common run of humanity. Before she has appeared, Bassanio is telling of the 'lady richly left', whose beauty draws suitors from all over the world to attempt the challenge of the caskets, and whose worth equals that of the famed Roman heroine of the same name. She may be too practical and too independent to fit the image of the fairy-tale princess, but could we describe Portia as an idealised character?

Portia will emerge as the judge and arbiter of the foolish world of men, and a formidable advocate of Christian morality, but she is not an unduly solemn character. Her first act in the play is to mock her various suitors, and we may still find a sense of mischief in her behaviour in Act 5. She is a dutiful daughter and obeys the strictures of her father's will, but her love for Bassanio is obvious and she makes little attempt at neutrality in the affair of the caskets.

Portia is quick to offer her support for Antonio and does not try to stop Bassanio returning to Venice. Indeed, secretly, she joins him disguised as a lawyer and proceeds to defend Antonio. She shows herself to be resourceful and commanding. She clearly and cleverly expounds the law, leading Shylock gently along the path towards his own destruction. By encouraging Shylock's utter determination to have just the letter of the law, justice without mercy, she opens the way for the same to be applied to him. However, Portia disregards her own eloquent plea about the quality of mercy when she sentences Shylock. When back in Belmont, she again demands the letter of the law from Bassanio in the ring plot, but then immediately shows him the mercy she did not show to Shylock in Venice.

Portia's love for Bassanio and, therefore, for his friend Antonio, overpowers Shylock's greed and defeats his deadly intent. Like Antonio and Bassanio, Portia demonstrates the power of love and friendship over greed.

Gratiano and Nerissa

Companion to Bassanio and Antonio, Gratiano 'speaks an infinite deal of nothing'; he is 'too wild, too rude, and bold of voice'. Despite the fact that he is not best suited to such a delicate mission, Gratiano is taken to Belmont by Bassanio (an action which demonstrates the strength of Bassanio's friendship). To a certain extent,

Gratiano acts as a contrast to Bassanio: note his more casual attitude to the ring plot and how, at the trial scene, he shows an ugly side when baiting the desperate Shylock. Bassanio's behaviour is more dignified and concerned.

Nerissa's role backs up Portia's. She joins Portia in the mockery of the suitors and provides support in all situations, notably the trial scene. Her words and actions often echo Portia's. The sense of 'echoing' is most apparent in Act 3, Scene 2 when, after the elaborate ceremony of the caskets, Gratiano and Nerissa announce that they, too, plan to marry: 'You saw the mistress, I beheld the maid.' In this way, their marriage both echoes and reinforces the love of Portia and Bassanio.

Jessica and Lorenzo

Shylock's daughter Jessica plays only a small part in the play. She demonstrates the power of love by being prepared to abandon not only her father but also her religion. Her desire to embrace Christianity would have been seen by Shakespeare's audience as a sign of moral excellence rather than an act of abandoning her faith. However, Jessica immediately offends against two of the Ten Commandments when she dishonours her father, by wishing she were not his daughter, and by stealing Shylock's money and jewels. Her casual use of Shylock's money, as reported by Tubal, infuriates Shylock and leads to the description of Shylock bemoaning his loss publicly, much to the amusement of all. This lessens the impact of what she has done and helps to bias the audience against her father.

Lorenzo's character is equally undeveloped. He functions from the start as one of a group of young Venetians who provide a common viewpoint on life and support for Antonio and Bassanio. However, he plays an important role with Jessica when left in charge at Belmont. The lyrical poetry of their scenes together epitomises the supremacy of love, and as such underpins a vital theme of the play.

About the author

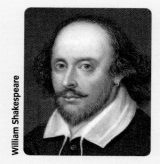

William Shakespeare

William Shakespeare was born in Stratford-upon-Avon, probably on 23 April 1564. His father, John Shakespeare, was a glove-maker by trade. John was a respected member of the community who held, at various times, several important public offices, including councillor, Justice of the Peace and, in 1568, Mayor. Besides his craft as a glover, he was a also successful businessman, trading in wool and involved in money lending. Shakespeare's mother, Mary Arden, was the daughter of a wealthy local farmer.

It is likely that, as the son of an important townsman, Shakespeare's education began at the town's 'petty' or junior school. He would then have progressed to Stratford Grammar School where he would have learned Latin and studied classical writers such as Ovid and Plautus. The influence of some of these writers can be seen in Shakespeare's plays, such as *Antony and Cleopatra* and *Julius Caeser*.

In 1582, when he was 18, Shakespeare married Anne Hathaway, the 26-year-old daughter of a local farmer. Their first child, Susanna, was born the following May and twins, Judith and Hamnet, were born two years later. Sadly, Hamnet died in 1596 at the age of eleven.

Very little is known about Shakespeare's life between 1585 and 1592, a period sometimes known as 'The Lost Years'. We do know, though, that by 1592 he had moved to London, probably leaving Stratford around 1586–87. No one knows why he left his home town, although one story suggests that he was caught poaching deer in the grounds of Sir Thomas Lucy and so left for London to avoid prosecution. However, it seems more likely that he joined one of the London-based theatre companies which sometimes visited Stratford. Shakespeare would have known that if he was to achieve success as an actor/playwright, London offered the best opportunities. By 1592 Shakespeare had established his reputation as an actor and dramatist and was sufficiently well-known to attract comment from some other dramatists of the time.

In 1593 all London theatres were closed because of the plague. When they re-opened the following year, Shakespeare had joined others in forming a new theatre company under the patronage of the Lord Chamberlain — called The Lord Chamberlain's Men. Shakespeare wrote plays for this company for almost 20 years and its leading actor, Richard Burbage, played many of his major roles, such as Hamlet, Othello and King Lear.

In 1599 the Lord Chamberlain's Men — with Shakespeare as a major shareholder — built a new theatre, The Globe, on the south bank of the Thames at Southwark. In 1603, following Queen Elizabeth's death, James I (James IV of Scotland) came to the throne. Shakespeare's company was extremely privileged in receiving his patronage and was allowed to changed its name to The King's Men. In 1609 the company acquired another theatre, the Blackfriars, in addition to The Globe.

Shakespeare's success had made him a wealthy man. As early as 1597 he had bought one of the biggest houses in Stratford, and he kept close links with his home town even though he lived in London. Shakespeare's father had been granted a coat of arms in 1596, and after his father's death in 1601 Shakespeare inherited this coat of arms and the rights of a gentleman, an unusual privilege for an actor or dramatist at the time.

During the early 1600s Shakespeare wrote some of his most famous tragedies, including *Hamlet*, *Othello*, *King Lear* and *Macbeth*, and his last plays — sometimes called the romances — which include *Cymbeline*, *The Tempest* and *The Winter's Tale*. In about 1611 Shakespeare seems to have left London and retired to Stratford a wealthy man, though he kept up his connection with London (he was involved in a legal dispute over the Blackfriars theatre in 1615). He died in Stratford on his birthday, 23 April 1616, and was buried there in the Holy Trinity Church.

Historical background

Theatre-going was very popular in Elizabethan England. Although the only permanent theatres were in London, theatre companies travelled throughout the country. Plays were regularly performed in temporary theatres created in inn yards, as well as at court and in the country houses of the wealthy. Shakespeare's plays, therefore, were seen by a wide range of people from all kinds of social backgrounds.

By the end of the Sixteenth Century, theatre-going was well established in England. However, the theatres and performances of Shakespeare's time were very different to their modern equivalents. The majority of the theatres, such as The Globe in Southwark, London, were open-air and, as there was no artificial lighting, the plays had to be performed in daylight, normally in the afternoons. The theatre itself was round or hexagonal in shape with a raised platform that jutted out into the audience. At the back of the stage, a kind of turret (supported by pillars and roofed) provided a high point from which a trumpeter signalled the beginning of the play and from which a flag flew, indicating that a performance was in progress.

The stage had no curtain and the main part of the audience stood around it on three sides. These sections of the audience were called the 'groundlings'. A few special members of the audience were allowed to sit on the stage itself. In the galleries, looking down on the stage and the groundlings, seating was provided for those who paid more to watch the play. These galleries were covered and so afforded protection from the weather.

At the back of the stage, a large tapestry or curtain was hung concealing a recess and openings at either side from which the actors could enter and exit. In a modern theatre, actors normally enter and exit from the sides or 'wings', but in Shakespeare's theatre entrances and exits were from the rear. The stage itself was covered and protected from the weather by a canopy which rested on posts or pillars at either side. There was usually at least one trap door in the stage itself, which could be used, for example, in the appearance or disappearance of a ghost. One of the galleries passed right over the back of the stage and, if required, it could be used in the action of the play itself, such as creating Juliet's balcony. Part of one of the lower galleries, to the side of the stage, was sometimes used by musicians who made a musical contribution to the play.

Behind the stage there were rooms called 'tiring rooms' in which the actors dressed and stored such props as were used. Although 'costumes' as we know them were not used, and actors dressed in the fashions of the times, these clothes were often more colourful or ornate and striking than those usually worn for everyday living. Painted scenery, too, was not used, but dark or colourful tapestries could reflect the mood of the play. Props, such as tables, chairs, cauldrons and swords were also important. All female roles were played by men or boys, as women were not allowed on the stage in Shakespeare's time.

Theatre-going was a very popular form of entertainment. The theatre was seen not only as a place to watch and enjoy a play, but also as a location in which to meet friends, exchange gossip and eat and drink. Elizabethan audiences were generally very knowledgeable about the theatre and were inclined to take an active part in the experience. They were appreciative of a good play performed well. However, if the play or performance was poor, they would often shout out derogatory remarks, make jokes at the actors' expense and throw things onto the stage — behaviour that is rarely seen at modern-day performances.

The Merchant of Venice remains one of Shakespeare's most popular plays.

Love versus greed

The play is a demonstration of the triumph of love and friendship over greed. The greed side of the equation is epitomised by Shylock. His conversations with first Bassanio and then Antonio show that he hates Christians mainly because they frustrate his money-making. Antonio, in particular, 'lends out money gratis, and brings down the rate of usance here in Venice', thus depriving Shylock of greater profit. When Jessica elopes and takes his money and jewels, it is the theft, rather than his daughter's fate, that concerns him. The trial scene epitomises the depths of Shylock's greed. Deaf to all pleas for mercy, he has his knife and scales ready to cut and weigh Antonio's flesh.

In contrast to Shylock's greed is the love and friendship demonstrated by Antonio, Bassanio and Portia. Antonio loves his friend Bassanio so much that he is prepared to put his life at the mercy of his enemy. Even without the payment of Shylock's forfeit, the loan hurts Antonio's heart because it takes Bassanio away from him. When writing to Bassanio to explain his predicament, Antonio requests only that he might have a last chance to see his friend before dying.

Bassanio knows that he can call upon Antonio's friendship to help him pursue Portia, even though he is already in debt to him. His friendship for Gratiano is also strong, and overcomes his better judgement when he agrees that they will both go to Belmont. He is honest in his love for Portia, which quickly overtakes his earlier sentiment: 'to get clear of all the debts I owe'. His love for Antonio brings him back to Venice where he offers his own life: 'The Jew shall have my flesh, blood, bones and all, / Ere thou shalt lose for me one drop of blood.' Bassanio's love for Portia makes him extremely reluctant to part with her ring, and he does so only when pressed by Antonio.

Portia's love for Bassanio extends to his friends. She offers her wealth to help Antonio, then departs in disguise for Venice in order to save his life. Finally, she forgives Bassanio for parting with her ring, reaffirming that love and forgiveness are superior to self-centred greed.

Mercy versus justice and the law

The trial scene (Act 4, Scene 1) is central to this aspect of the play. As it opens, the Duke judges Shylock 'an inhuman wretch, / Uncapable of pity, void, and empty / From any dram of mercy'. Nevertheless, mercy is precisely what the Duke asks Shylock to show. Crucially, when Shylock has rejected many more ducats than called for by the bond, the Duke wonders: 'How shalt thou hope for mercy, rend'ring none?' It is here that the court's merciless persecution of Shylock, once he has lost his case, finds some of its justification.

Portia's main speech in this scene extols the virtue of mercy: 'The quality of mercy is not strain'd'. Cleverly, her aim is to lead Shylock to reiterate his demand for law and justice. When she suggests that a surgeon should be present to stop the blood so that Antonio does not bleed to death, Shylock objects that this was not part of the bond. But the simple, blind administration of the law which is what Shylock wants will not give him his revenge or Antonio's life: instead, and without mercy, it takes from him his wealth and his religion. Portia is as merciless as Shylock in her administration of the law. Antonio shows mercy, as does the Duke. It is therefore important that, when Portia returns to Belmont, she demonstrates both forgiveness of and mercy for Bassanio.

Race and racism

Arguments over Shakespeare's attitude to race in *The Merchant of Venice* still rage. Some people suggest that such an anti-Semitic text should not be taught in schools; others claim that the play is an attack on prejudice. There are many reasons for this confusion, apart from the usual difficulties over interpretation of characters (a particular problem with Shylock).

It is important to realise that the Jewish community had suffered huge prejudice since the Middle Ages. Jews were accused on many trumped-up charges, massacres of Jews occurred, and eventually, in 1290, the entire community was expelled from England and not re-admitted until the mid-seventeenth century. Astonishingly, therefore, in Shakespeare's time Jews were totally banned from living in England. In some European countries the same applied; in other places (including Venice) Jews lived in ghettos — separate, walled parts of the city which were locked at night. The portrayal of Shylock as a money-lender also has its basis in historical fact. Jews had become associated with this profession over many centuries, as Christians were not allowed to lend money at interest to other Christians.

Shakespeare's portrayal of Shylock and Tubal is therefore based on common prejudice and intolerance tempered by his own liberal tolerance. Thus he can imagine Shylock making a plea as a human being, but cannot fully escape the stereotype. We must also remember that, living at a time of fiercely held Christian views, Shakespeare naturally (if wrongly) thinks that converting to Christianity is a good choice for a Jew.

It is also difficult, for the above reasons, to determine what the characters' racial prejudice is intended to reveal about them. Prejudice against the Jews can be seen as part of the character of a rather loud-mouthed young man (Gratiano at the trial) and of a mature and honourable figure like Antonio.

Perhaps the most disturbing thing for a modern audience is the lack of concern for what happens to Shylock. Note that he is not the only character in Shakespeare's plays to be tricked, mocked and allowed to depart furious and defeated (think of Malvolio in *Twelfth Night*). Another sign of how far Shakespeare humanises the stereotype is that the audience cares about what happens to Shylock, even if the characters do not.

Disguise

Disguise offers female characters in Shakespeare's plays liberation and the opportunity to experience a completely different lifestyle. Portia and Nerissa disguise themselves as a lawyer and a clerk. They are thus able to enter the male-dominated Venice and are empowered sufficiently to make a difference. As a woman, Portia would not have been able to bring Shylock to justice and save Antonio's life. They are also able to play a trick on their new husbands and demand the rings they have promised never to part with. Jessica, too, disguises herself as a boy in order to escape her father and elope with Lorenzo. Her disguise enables her to escape undetected and flee without being questioned. You should also consider the relevance of theatrical conventions in determining plot. In Shakespeare's theatre, all female roles were played by boys. Storylines involving disguises to conceal gender therefore gain an added comic dimenesion.

The pound of flesh bond

Antonio enters into a bond with Shylock. In return for 3000 ducats, he agrees to repay the money within three months or allow Shylock to cut a pound of flesh from anywhere on his body. His ventures seem to fail and Shylock claims his forfeit. In court, Shylock's desire for the law rebounds on him, and he loses all.

The casket test

Portia's father has decreed in his will that she must marry the man who selects the correct one of three caskets made of gold, silver and lead. He judged that Portia would love a man who can distinguish between apparent worth and real worth. Bassanio chooses the correct casket, lead, and marries Portia.

The ring bond

When Portia and Nerissa marry, they give rings to their husbands, who swear never to part with them. After the trial, both men are persuaded to give the rings to the lawyer and his clerk. Returning to Belmont, Portia and Nerissa ask where their rings are. They accuse their husbands of being unfaithful to their vows, but finally reveal their plot. Bassanio and Gratiano are then shown the mercy that Shylock is not afforded.

Text commentary

Act 1

Act 1, Scene 1

> *In sooth I know not why I am so sad.*

'What stuff 'tis made of, whereof it is born, I am to learn'. No reason is given here or later for <u>Antonio's sadness</u>. Almost certainly his love for and close friendship with Bassanio will be affected by the latter's pursuit of Portia. This is not a homosexual relationship, but there is no doubt that <u>the friendship of Bassanio provides a large part of Antonio's emotional life</u>. Antonio is only seen in the company of younger men who respect him for his honour and generosity, and the end of the play suggests a man who has lost his role. However, another possible reason for his sadness is the <u>Elizabethan fashion for 'melancholy'</u>: there is a suggestion that it is partly assumed, as hinted by Gratiano later. The 'want-wit' that Antonio accuses himself of in this scene will, in a way, be fulfilled when he enters into the bond with Shylock.

Explore

Antonio's character is ambiguous from the start. If he cannot understand himself, how can the audience?

The words of Solanio and Salerio, where they stress the dangers and worries of being in Antonio's position, are very prophetic. However, Antonio gives three reasons why his ventures do not worry him: his goods are not all in one ship, nor are they concentrated in one place, and the results of this year's trading will not decide the fate of his fortunes. Nevertheless, <u>the idea that his ships may be endangered is firmly planted in this scene</u>. Also note that Antonio does not make his two friends aware of how short of money he is — a fact that he will disclose only to Bassanio.

Antonio rejects the suggestion that he is in love, and so we still have no good explanation for his sadness. Note how speedily (and perhaps contemptuously) Antonio dismisses the idea of being in love: what might that suggest to you about his character and relationships? <u>His sadness acts as a foil for the lightheartedness of his companions</u>. In a similar way, Antonio's trial will act as a background and contrast to the various romances.

Salerio (in some editions, Salarino) and Solanio are not important characters, but <u>they serve a useful and effective choric role</u>. The Chorus in Greek tragedy (often a group of elders or townspeople) informed the audience of matters of which they were ignorant, and commented on characters and their situations. Salerio and Solanio seem to be representatives of their society: their almost interchangeable names suggest that <u>they are types, not individuals</u>.

Explore

Work out how Salerio and Solanio act as a Chorus here.

> ❝*A stage, where every man must play a part,*
> *And mine a sad one.*❞

Antonio's words to Gratiano, restate his feelings and reflect events to come. At almost every turn misfortune dogs him, and even at the end, when Shylock loses his case and his ships return home, <u>Antonio stands apart from the love and happiness that his companions enjoy</u>.

Gratiano's comment, <u>'Let me play the fool'</u>, finds its reflection in others' opinions of him. Bassanio's assessment of Gratiano is that he <u>'speaks an infinite deal of nothing'</u>, but the friendship between the two overcomes Bassanio's judgement when put to the test later in the play. Gratiano is also tactless — he has to be dragged away by Lorenzo to allow Bassanio and Antonio to talk privately. Bassanio gives further comments on Gratiano's character in Act 2, Scene 2.

Explore

Do you think Antonio's sadness is related to affectation and vanity?

However, foolish chatterer though Gratiano appears to be, he has a point to make. He talks to Antonio about men who '<u>are</u> <u>reputed</u> <u>wise</u>' simply because they do not speak, and those who become <u>self-consciously</u> <u>solemn</u> <u>and</u> <u>silent</u> to gain credit for 'wisdom [and] gravity'.

When Gratiano departs, Antonio immediately taxes Bassanio with a question about the 'secret pilgrimage' to a lady. Perhaps here lies the secret of Antonio's sadness. His <u>friendship</u> <u>with</u> <u>Bassanio</u> <u>is</u> <u>obviously</u> <u>very</u> <u>close</u>, and maybe it is the thought of losing that closeness which makes him sad.

Bassanio ignores Antonio's question and launches straight into an account of his money problems. The 'secret pilgrimage' turns into a way '<u>to</u> <u>get</u> <u>clear</u> <u>of</u> <u>all</u> <u>the</u> <u>debts</u> I <u>owe</u>'. Be aware, however, that while this is an immediate consideration for Bassanio, <u>it</u> <u>is</u> <u>not</u> <u>his</u> <u>sole</u> <u>reason</u> <u>for</u> <u>pursuing</u> <u>Portia:</u> <u>he</u> <u>does</u> <u>love</u> <u>her</u>. To Elizabethans, the idea of marrying for fortune was not unusual, nor was it a practice to be condemned. That Bassanio feels able to turn to his friend for a loan demonstrates the closeness of their relationship and the extent to which <u>money</u> <u>becomes</u> <u>subservient</u> <u>to</u> <u>love</u>. Note the way that Antonio is willing to help him even though to an extent he will lose Bassanio as a result.

Bassanio wants to borrow money to 'woo' a rich heiress. Money is a theme that features in the relationships of all the characters in the play. <u>Venice,</u> the setting, is a centre of <u>wealth,</u> <u>trade,</u> <u>money-lending</u> <u>and</u> <u>greed</u>, and here the drama of love versus greed and mercy versus justice is played out.

Bassanio is more than just a good-hearted spendthrift, as events will show. Here, his conversation with Antonio indicates that <u>he is embarrassed at having to ask for yet more money</u>, so does not come straight to the point.

> ## *In Belmont is a lady richly left*

There is little of nobility in this opening scene: idle, joking young men, a melancholic merchant and his friend seeking his usual loan. <u>With the mention of Portia, however, poetry and romance enter</u>. 'In Belmont is a lady richly left' is a line suggestive of the old romances: throughout the play you will find hints of <u>Belmont as an other-worldly place</u>. Portia is introduced as being on a different plane from the other characters.

Explore

Portia is compared to another Portia: Cato's daughter, Brutus' wife. See what you can find out about her, possibly from Shakespeare's *Julius Caesar*.

It is in this scene that the events leading to the strange bond agreement between Antonio and Shylock have their origins. Antonio reacts sharply to Bassanio's attempt to justify his request for yet another loan. This indicates the great depth of Antonio's love — in his eyes, Bassanio should never have been in any doubt that he would get his loan.

<u>Venice and Belmont are places of contrast</u>. Here we see Venice as the seat of trade and money. It is where greed, usury and revenge will play their ugly parts. Love will find its fulfilment in Belmont. In Venice, Antonio's love for Bassanio will be frustrated, but perversely it is Venice's money which will help Bassanio's love on its way.

Act 1, Scene 2

> ## *my little body is aweary of this great world*

For the first half of the play, linked plots develop simultaneously in Venice and Belmont, with Bassanio the connection between them. One is the story of Antonio's bond, the other the story of Portia's suitors. Later in the play the two plots will become more closely intertwined.

Explore

Is Portia's behaviour here like a 'fairy-tale princess'? Look at the way she and Nerissa discuss the suitors. Is there a deliberate contrast of earnestness and humour?

After the world of business in Venice, Portia's situation seems almost unreal: there are <u>hints of the fairy-tale princess</u> in her castle besieged by lovers who have to undergo a trial to win her hand. Here in Belmont, the concerns are not those of the merchants but of a father's desire for his daughter's happiness; rather different from Shylock's major interest — profit. But <u>Portia is wearied by the thought that she might be forced to marry someone whom she does not love</u>, and by the uncertainty this causes.

Note that the two locations are distinct: <u>Belmont is a place of music and love; Venice a place of greed and threatened disaster.</u>

> ❝ *I may neither choose who I would, nor refuse who I dislike* ❞

Explore

Compare and contrast Portia's father's love for his daughter with Shylock's love for Jessica.

Portia discusses her father's will with her maid and companion, Nerissa. The will requires any suitor to choose between three caskets made from lead, silver and gold. Again the idea of wealth features, in that judgements are to be made about value and worth, but in this case the judgements also relate to love. The suitors have their own views as to whose worth is being judged, theirs or Portia's. This <u>casket bond</u> (for a bond is what the will amounts to) <u>echoes the pound of flesh bond</u> that will be entered into by Antonio. However, the bond between father and daughter has only love and happiness as its motivating force, while the bond between Shylock and Antonio has hatred and revenge on Shylock's part, and love for his friend on Antonio's part.

Portia and Nerissa discuss the various dignitaries who have visited Belmont and desired to marry Portia. Portia's assessment of the men's characters shows her as <u>perceptive</u> <u>and</u> <u>incisively</u> <u>witty</u>, with a sharp eye for detail. When she takes up Antonio's case later in the play she demonstrates a great deal of mental agility and competence.

<u>The</u> <u>brief</u> <u>reference</u> <u>to</u> <u>Bassanio</u> <u>lets</u> <u>the</u> <u>audience</u> <u>know</u> <u>that</u> <u>Portia</u> <u>favours</u> <u>him</u>: 'I remember him well, and I remember him worthy of thy praise.' Bassanio is the only suitor whom Portia takes seriously. There are many areas of tension in *The Merchant of Venice*, but the result of his wooing is not one of them.

Act 1, Scene 3

❝ *Three thousand ducats, well.* **❞**

The bond, whereby Antonio will borrow three thousand ducats that become repayable after three months, is negotiated by Bassanio. Shylock admits that Antonio is probably a 'good man' for the loan: <u>his</u> <u>use</u> <u>of</u> <u>the</u> <u>word</u> <u>'good'</u> <u>relates</u> <u>only</u> <u>to</u> <u>Antonio's</u> <u>ability</u> <u>to</u> <u>pay</u>. However, he comments on the fact that Antonio's ships carry his wealth, and are easy prey to the perils of sea and man.

Before the scene starts, Bassanio has made his request and Shylock appears to be considering it like a careful businessman. The character of Shylock can be presented in many different ways. The Elizabethan audience would have expected <u>a</u> <u>stereotypical</u> <u>monster</u> <u>of</u> <u>greed</u>; until the nineteenth century there was a tradition of presenting him as <u>a</u> <u>villain</u>; this was followed by another tradition of presenting Shylock as <u>noble</u> <u>victim.</u>

Shakespeare's presentation, however, is more balanced and subtle than any of these interpretations.

Explore

What does this speech demonstrate about Shylock's relationship with Christians?

Shylock summarises his approach to Christians generally just before Antonio's entrance, when he explains what he will do with Christians ('I will buy with you') and what he refuses to do ('I will not eat with you'). <u>His attitude to Antonio in particular is one of hatred</u>, for various reasons, but is based on two particular complaints: Antonio hates Jews and he lends money without interest.

<u>Both Antonio and Shylock are outsiders</u>. Shylock is spurned by the Christians, and Antonio is often alone, in contrast to the loves being pursued by his companions. They clearly show their hatred for each other. The speech beginning 'Signior Antonio, many a time and oft', demonstrates the depth of feeling that underpins their antagonism towards each other.

Since Antonio sees himself as an honourable man, you should note that he confirms Shylock's accusations: 'call thee so *again*', 'spit on thee *again*'. <u>Shylock's accusations are justified</u>.

Antonio uses Shylock's hatred as bait to persuade him to make the loan — not that he needs much persuasion. After all, Antonio suggests, if the money is not repaid Shylock may exact a forfeit with an easy conscience since it is his enemy who has failed to fulfil the terms of the agreement. Bearing in mind Shylock's recent speech, we must be suspicious of his motives when he suddenly declares, '<u>I would be friends with you, and have your love</u>'.

> ❝ *Yes, Shylock I will seal unto this bond.* ❞

The penalty, or forfeit, to be exacted if Antonio fails to repay the three thousand ducats in three months' time is now explained by

Shylock: a pound of flesh to be cut from any part of Antonio's body that Shylock wishes.

Bassanio recognises the dangers of the forfeit and protests that no agreement should be made. However, Antonio is convinced that his ships will return in time and that he will be able to repay the bond. No doubt his love for Bassanio also clouds his judgement in this matter. Bassanio bows to Antonio's determination to help him. Shylock's comment that 'To buy his favour, I extend this friendship' is not only false in its declared intention but also fundamentally at odds with the reality of friendship/love — by its very nature it cannot be bought, only given.

Explore

Look at different film versions of this scene. Which side is the audience intended to be on and why?

Antonio's comments about Shylock becoming a Christian and growing kind ('gentle' is a pun on 'gentile', meaning non-Jew) completely misinterpret Shylock's motives and attitudes. Ironically, the 'Hebrew will turn Christian' (see the trial scene) — but not willingly.

A major theme that runs through the play relates to the fact that things are not always as they seem to be. In particular, we have just seen how Shylock has 'talked down' the significance of the pound of flesh forfeit, and how he says he wishes to buy Antonio's favour. The reality is that he sees the forfeit as a real threat to Antonio's life and has absolutely no desire for his friendship. This theme is central to all the bonds in the play. Shylock really wants to profit from Antonio's death as he will be able to charge higher rates of interest when Antonio can no longer undercut him. The metal from which each casket is made disguises the reality of what it contains. The rings are not given away to strangers: in reality they stay with the married couples. Antonio offers his final bond for Bassanio thinking his friend needs support when really there is no need.

Text commentary

Quick quiz 1

Uncover the plot

Delete two of the three alternatives given to find the correct plot. Beware possible misconceptions and muddles.

Antonio/Bassanio/Gratiano is the Merchant of Venice. He owes lots of money/has money tied up in trade/wants to marry a rich heiress, and goes to the moneylender Tubal/Launcelot Gobbo/Shylock to borrow three thousand pounds/six thousand ducats/three thousand ducats for his friend Stephano/Salanio/Bassanio. It is agreed that if the money is not repaid in six months/three months/one month, the forfeit will be 'thrice three times the value of this bond'/'three chests of gold, sliver and lead'/'an equal pound of your fair flesh'.

Who? What? Where? When? Why?

1   Who will be the 'weeping philosopher when he grows old?'
2   Who would Portia rather shrive her than wive her?
3   Who looks like 'a fawning publican'?
4   Who urges a 'childlike proof' to Antonio?
5   Who cites the Scriptures and how is he described?
6   Who 'caught it, found it, or came by it'? What was it?
7   Who are the 'parcel of wooers'?
8   What is the 'merry sport'?
9   What is 'A stage, where every man must play a part'?
10   What was the 'childlike proof'?

Open quotes

Find the line — and complete the phrase or sentence.

1   'My ventures are not…'
2   'To buy his favour…'
3   'I will feed fat…'

Act 2

Act 2, Scene 1

66 *Mislike me not for my complexion* 99

The theme of appearance versus reality is central to the casket bond plotline. The very first words of the Prince of Morocco ask that he should not be 'misliked' for his colour. He declares his blood is redder than that of any man from a northern climate. The Prince of Morocco is arrogant and self-centred, impressed by outward appearance. He is also presented as being exotic and foreign, with references to his scimitar and the sultan, but again Shakespeare preserves the racial balance. The Prince may be an object of some mockery, but it is not because of his 'complexion': the other suitors receive similar treatment and he is noble, dignified and educated.

Portia, in response, makes it known that she has no real choice in the matter of what he does, but that he is as good as any she has looked on so far. Her comment that her father had 'scanted me, / And hedged me by his wit' suggests that she has carefully considered the conditions and has decided they are watertight. She will not break the conditions of this or any other agreement.

As with the bond between Shylock and Antonio, there is a forfeit if the incorrect casket is chosen. However, this is Belmont, a place where love and music hold sway, and the forfeit reflects this fact. Should the wrong casket be chosen, the suitor may never 'speak to lady afterward / In way of marriage'. A hard condition but, within the context of the play, one that emphasises the importance of love and the fact that a loving relationship should not be entered into lightly.

> **Certainly my conscience will serve me to run from this Jew my master.**

Launcelot's comic soliloquy at the start of the scene presents a 'difficult' decision for him — if he stays in Shylock's service, he stays with 'the devil'; if he obeys the 'fiend' and goes to Bassanio, he will offend just the same. The reality is that he has no choice. If Bassanio will have him as a servant then he will join him. Here starts the process by which <u>Shylock</u> <u>will</u> <u>gradually</u> <u>be</u> <u>stripped</u> <u>of</u> <u>all</u> <u>he</u> <u>has</u>: servant, daughter, wealth, religion.

Old Gobbo cannot recognise his own son and Launcelot disguises the truth from him for a short while. The confusion between the correct use of various words: 'infection', 'defect', 'impertinent', etc. reflects Shylock's own misuse of the words 'good', 'favour' and 'friendship'. These distortions also bring to mind Antonio's confusion over the Jew's 'kindness'.

<u>The</u> <u>Shakespearean</u> <u>acting</u> <u>company</u> <u>always</u> <u>contained</u> <u>at</u> <u>least</u> <u>one</u> <u>clown</u>, who was usually cast in a part which offered scope for song, dance and improvised gags. Launcelot plays a cruel joke on his blind father by not admitting his identity: what is the effect when later Old Gobbo refuses to accept that he is his son? Interestingly, what seems likely to be used as a comic double act never develops later in the play.

Explore

Think what this contradiction of wealth and lifestyle shows about the characters of Shylock and Bassanio. It probably reflects credit on neither of them.

Bassanio disputes whether it is promotion to leave 'a rich Jew's service' to work for 'so poor a gentleman'. On the other hand, Bassanio's table is 'fairer' by far than Shylock's and he spends much more freely.

Given the importance and delicate nature of Bassanio's visit to Belmont and the amount it has cost his friend Antonio, one

Text commentary

might wonder at the sense of allowing a person of such 'wild behaviour' as Gratiano to accompany him. What it does underline is the strength of the bonds of friendship and love that these Venetians have for each other. <u>Cold calculations of profit and gain do not enter into the matter when friendship is at stake</u>.

Act 2, Scene 3

66 *I am sorry thou wilt leave my father so.* 99

Jessica acquaints us with her unhappiness at home. The fact that Shylock is a lone figure in the play is underlined by the fact that even his own daughter rejects him. <u>Jessica is ashamed of her ancestry</u>. Ironically, both Jessica and Shylock will become Christians, but for very different reasons.

Act 2, Scene 4

66 *Nay, we will slink away in suppertime.* 99

Lorenzo, Gratiano, Solanio and Salerio (Salarino) are preparing for the masque being held by Bassanio. Launcelot arrives with Jessica's message and Lorenzo promises he will not fail her. He tells Gratiano of their plans. Jessica has directed that she will leave her father's house <u>disguised as a page</u>. She will also take Shylock's gold and jewels.

Explore

What do you think about the justice of Jessica's actions and what the young Christians are doing to assist her in theft?

According to the morals of the play, Shylock should have been able to give his daughter both <u>his love and his wealth</u>. The one thing that cannot be stolen by his daughter, which is worth far more than material things, he does not give her at all — his love. His wealth, which he values above all, she steals.

Act 2, Scene 5

❝*Lock up my doors*❞

Shylock leaves Jessica in charge of his house with strict instructions to keep it and his goods secure. Ironically, while he is gone she will first take his wealth and then, in disguise, elope with Lorenzo. In a later and parallel scene, Jessia and Lorenzo are left in charge of Portia's house. But that will be in Belmont, and the only thing that happens there is that Lorenzo and Jessica's love for each other grows — certainly no one's house will be robbed.

Shylock's determination to 'go in hate to feed upon / The prodigal Christian' reminds us of the prejudice and hatred in his character. His account of his dreams makes him slightly comic. Any sympathy the audience might have for him and the fate he will suffer at his daughter's hands is swept away by his own words and attitudes. (Shylock is right to worry about his 'money bags'.) He shows his hatred for the Venetians and their music: contrast this to the atmosphere in Belmont. His concern with profit colours all his actions, as is evidenced by his reference to Launcelot as being 'snail-slow in profit'.

Act 2, Scene 6

❝*Descend, for you must be my torchbearer.*❞

Jessica, disguised as a boy, elopes with Lorenzo, taking Shylock's money and jewels with her. Shylock's distrust of the masques ('Christian fools with varnish'd faces'), expressed in the previous scene, has proved well-founded. This is an interesting scene in that we are presented with the uncomfortable knowledge that

Jessica, with whom we are surely meant to sympathise, <u>breaks two of the Ten Commandments</u> by which Christians should order their lives: she fails to honour her father and she steals.

Against her actions are to be balanced the audience's dislike of Shylock and Jessica's own hatred of him. The light-hearted tone of the scene and the obvious love of Lorenzo for Jessica help us perhaps to consider her actions in a more forgiving light. Interestingly, Jessica says to Lorenzo, <u>'catch this casket; it is worth the pains'</u>.

Explore

Look more closely at Jessica's situation. Does she have conflicting loyalties here?

Note Gratiano's comments on how <u>the outcome of events often belies the original expectations</u>. Perhaps most ominous is his reference to ships that return 'lean, rent, and beggared by the strumpet wind', placing Antonio's risk in the context of Shylock's daughter eloping with a Christian — Shylock's anger may well be vented on Antonio.

Antonio's arrival with the news that the wind has shifted and that Bassanio is about to depart reintroduces the casket bond and moves us smoothly back to Belmont.

Act 2, Scene 7

> ❝ *Who chooseth me shall gain what many men desire.* ❞

You must be clear about the inscriptions on each casket. Note how they talk of what men 'desire' and 'deserve', and of giving and hazarding all one has. There is a link here between the casket bond and the pound of flesh bond. Shylock desires gold, but one might consider that eventually he gets what he deserves. Antonio is a merchant and presumably also pursues gold, but he is willing to hazard all that he has for things that Shylock presumably would consider worthless and profitless: friendship and love.

The extent to which this is <u>a test of various philosophies of life</u> is made clear by the lengthy speeches by which Morocco and Arragon make their decision and explain their reasons. The Prince rejects the lead casket: 'Hazard for lead!' Its appearance disguises, for him, the reality of what it contains. He uses the wrong standards by which to judge it.

> **"All that glisters is not gold"**

At first the Prince finds it difficult to choose between the silver and gold caskets. He believes he deserves Portia, but he cannot reconcile the differences in external value between silver and gold. The contrasts in wealth that they represent lead him inexorably towards <u>choosing the appearance of wealth and riches</u>. Note that this is a path that Shylock has followed and which has lost him his wealth and his daughter. The Prince is as much concerned with his own worth and what he deserves as with the worth of the caskets and what they represent.

The contents of the gold casket, <u>a skull and a scroll</u>, dramatically highlight the distinction between the appearance of the casket and the reality of what is inside: <u>'Gilded tombs do worms infold'</u> vividly captures the pointlessness of fascination with wealth.

Act 2, Scene 8

> **"Justice! the law! My ducats and my daughter!"**

From the Prince of Morocco's disappointment caused by his choice of the gold that 'glisters' we move swiftly back to Venice and hear of Shylock's utter dismay at the loss of his gold and jewels: <u>the Jew's home is as empty of wealth as Morocco's casket was of Portia</u>. Solanio's impersonation of Shylock voices his major concerns:

his jewels, his ducats, his daughter and justice. <u>Shylock is portrayed as a laughable figure</u>. You may think that the comical variations on the theme of 'ducats' and 'daughter' are the result of Solanio's mocking dislike for Shylock, but it seems that he is not exaggerating.

Again there is talk of Antonio's ships being at risk, and the warning that he should beware Shylock's hatred or else he will be made to pay for the Jew's woe. The description of the parting of Bassanio and Antonio again highlights their love and friendship for each other and the extent to which Antonio is prepared to sacrifice his wealth and well-being for Bassanio: '<u>I think he only loves the world for him.</u>' He even goes so far as to counsel Bassanio not to worry about the time it may take to win Portia's hand. This part of the scene again provides <u>a strong contrast between the concerns of Shylock and Antonio</u>. For the former the focus is ducats and jewels; for the latter, love for a friend. At the same time, Antonio is not totally an admirable character — here we may question his sense of proportion.

Act 2, Scene 9

> *Who chooseth me shall get as much as he deserves.*

The Prince dismisses the lead casket with hardly a second glance. Reading the warning on the lead casket that he must be prepared to '<u>give and hazard all he hath</u>', the Prince cannot bring himself to consider such a sacrifice for 'base lead'. Having arrogantly dismissed the lead casket because of its apparent low worth, he ironically dismisses the gold because the 'fool multitude' would 'choose by show' — the very fault he demonstrated when rejecting the lead casket. His choice demonstrates both his low opinion of others and the high opinion he holds of himself.

Explore

Look at the rhymes and Arragon's reaction. Both Morocco and Arragon are proud men, valuing themselves too highly: which do you think is the prouder of the two?

The contents of the silver casket are <u>a fool's head and a scroll</u>. The scroll's words say that his 'desert' is a mere shadow, something 'silvered' but only overlaid, not solid. The Prince has been a fool, and the fool's head is appropriate for a person of such vanity. The scene proceeds very much on the lines of the scene with Morocco, but you might find a slightly more bitter and mocking mood.

Explore

Arragon's self-love and view of a wife as possession are condemned. Note how Bassanio passes the test but also has friendship and love for Portia.

The news that Bassanio has arrived links the worlds of Belmont and Venice. Portia comments a little warily on the enthusiasm with which his arrival is announced, but Nerissa seems to be sure of what she wants: <u>'Bassanio, Lord Love, if thy will it be!'</u>

By the end of Act 2, many of the essential elements are in place, and <u>it will only take a few incidents to transform the situations, intentions and security of the characters:</u>

- The bond of friendship between Antonio and Bassanio and the hatred between Shylock and Antonio have been established.

- The pound of flesh bond between Antonio and Shylock has been entered into.

- Antonio's ships are reported to be in danger.

- Bassanio's wish to marry Portia has put Antonio's life in danger, but their marriage will eventually save his life.

- Shylock's daughter rejects him and his religion, and steals his money and jewels.

- Portia, evidently intelligent and witty, submits to her father's will and abides by his decrees as to how she should find a husband.

Uncover the plot

Delete two of the three alternatives given to find the correct plot. Beware possible misconceptions and muddles.

In Belmont/Venice/Morocco, the casket bond proceeds: with two suitors already rejected, news comes that the Prince of Morocco/Bassanio/Prince of Arragon is at Portia's gate. Meanwhile, Shylock is left bewailing the loss of 'my servant and my daughter'/'my daughter and my jewels'/'my ducats and my daughter'. His servant Launcelot/Lorenzo/Leonardo has left him for Bassanio, and his daughter Nerissa/Jessica/Portia has eloped with Lorenzo — and the treasure. There is, however, some news that will gladden Shylock's heart: 'she hath the stones upon her and the ducats'/'all that glisters is not gold'/'there miscarried a vessel of our country richly fraught'.

Who? What? Where? When? Why?

1   Who is 'a huge feeder / Snail-slow in profit'?

2   Who is asked 'to allay with some cold drops of modesty / Thy skipping spirit', and by whom?

3   What is Jessica to wear for her elopement, and what role will she play?

4   What *three* promises attend the choice of the wrong casket?

5   What does Shylock cry for in the streets?

6   Where did Shylock first go when he discovered his loss?

7   Where was Shylock while Jessica escaped his house?

8   Why does Shylock have a sense of 'ill a-brewing'?

9   Why is Shylock particularly happy to let Launcelot go to Bassanio's household?

10   Why does the Prince of Morocco fear Portia will 'mislike' him?

Act 3

Act 3, Scene 1

> ❝*Now, what news on the Rialto?*❞

The Act opens in Venice with the news that one of Antonio's ships is reported to have been sunk. Then Shylock enters. His concern that his daughter has fled is a source of entertainment to Salerio and Solanio. Note that they draw a clear distinction between Shylock and Jessica. She may have been born to him and be of his race, but in reality she is no more akin to him than is Portia.

> ❝*If you prick us, do we not bleed?*❞

In this well-known speech, Shylock first lists the wrongs that he says Antonio has done him, and then considers the <u>similarities</u> <u>between</u> <u>Christians</u> <u>and</u> <u>Jews</u> — they are both human, with the

same 'organs, dimensions, senses, affections, passions'. Shylock's <u>eloquence</u> can be powerful and moving at times, and it is certainly so here. In powerful, simple oratory, with very effective use of repetition, he stresses the common humanity of Jew and Gentile/Christian. This is a message that both Jews and Christians often forget in this play, and Shylock himself soon turns to thoughts of revenge.

Explore

Do you think there is any truth in Shylock's claim that he has learned villainy from the Christians?

Shylock's words, which should be a plea for mercy, turn ironically to the exact opposite. He will seek justice (revenge), not mercy. This speech helps to prepare us for his virulent pursuit of the bond's forfeit. Shakespeare's ideals remain Christian virtues, even when the Christian characters he creates can be sadly lacking in them.

Any sympathy the audience might have for Shylock as a result of his impassioned speech quickly evaporates as they listen to him rail against his daughter. His only concerns are for his ducats, his jewels and now, more ominously, his revenge.

Tubal's report that one of Antonio's ships has been sunk is greeted by Shylock with great happiness. Along with everyone else, Tubal seems to delight in teasing Shylock. By the end of the scene, any sympathy that Shylock might have gained is effectively negated by the spectacle of him being mischievously tortured by Tubal, showing him at his worst. Tubal first reminds Shylock that Jessica is spending his money, but then balances that bad news by talking about Antonio's creditors, who worry they will not be paid. Then, swiftly, he tells of a ring which Jessica has sold, one given to Shylock by his wife; but then, again, he reassures Shylock that 'Antonio is certainly undone'.

Note that throughout this scene Shylock's only concern is for himself. <u>He sees himself as a suffering representative of his people</u>: 'The curse never fell upon our nation till now'. This elevates his suffering above that of all the Jews persecuted over the centuries: an identification with his race, but a very selfish one. His final words to Tubal, 'were [Antonio] out of Venice, I can make what merchandise I will', summarise his purpose in pursuing 'justice' against Antonio; and of making profit through revenge.

Act 3, Scene 2

> ❝I pray you tarry, pause a day or two❞

Portia's plea to Bassanio shows how much she wishes him to be successful and that she is worried he might choose the wrong casket. <u>'One half of me is yours'</u>: the concept of giving totally is repeated here. Portia loves Bassanio, but <u>her desire for him will not drive</u>

her to break the bond imposed by her father, even though she might lose Bassanio because of it.

Portia's determination to live within the letter of the law is demonstrated again later in the play when she declines Bassanio's invitation at the trial: 'To do a great right, do a little wrong.' Her answer, 'many an error by the same sample will rush into the state', shows how clearly she sees the evil consequences which may follow such an action. Note how her attitude parallels that of Antonio, who shows a similar determination to be bound by the law, regardless of the consequences for himself, when he is called upon to honour the pound of flesh bond.

Portia has faith in her father's will. She realises that if Bassanio loves her he will not be distracted by the appearances of the caskets as her other suitors were.

❝*Let music sound* **❞**

Portia commands that music be played while Bassanio makes his choice. Belmont is a place of love, friendship and happiness, where Portia will find her husband. It is fitting that music should accompany Bassanio's choice. Her command is in striking contrast to Shylock's response to music in Act 2, Scene 5: 'the vile squealing'.

In five lines, Bassanio encapsulates major elements of the play:
'So may the outward shows be least themselves;
The world is still deceived with ornament.
In law, what plea so tainted and corrupt
But, being season'd with a gracious voice,
Obscures the show of evil?'

The appearance of things has little to do with their reality and so Bassanio will not be deceived by the worth of the metals from which the caskets are made. This quotation also has relevance for Shylock's desire for 'justice', which is really a quest first for revenge and then for profit once Antonio is dead. Again, the 'plea so tainted and corrupt' aptly describes Shylock's 'do we not bleed' speech, and looks forward to Shylock's plea for justice and law at Antonio's trial.

> **Who chooseth me, must give and hazard all he hath.**

Bassanio devotes some time to exploring the contradictions between appearance and reality, and his final words, 'The seeming truth which cunning times put on / To entrap the wisest', lead logically and correctly to his rejection of the gold and silver caskets. His correct choice of the lead casket is greeted with joy by Portia and they both talk of their willingness to give all to each other and of their unworthiness to receive each other's love.

The giving of the ring symbolises all of Portia's possessions, given freely to Bassanio. However, as with all bonds there is a forfeit to be paid if it is broken. Here in Belmont, the bond and forfeit are not based on money but on love and giving. However, with the resolution of the casket bond, the creation of this new bond serves to remind us that another has yet to run its course — the pound of flesh bond.

Bassanio's friendship with Gratiano seems to have had a good effect. The marriage between Gratiano and Nerissa is announced —— surely another lesson in how true love and friendship, the willingness to give all, brings its own reward. In contrast, Shylock will lose all.

The arrival of the party from Venice completes the group of happy lovers. However, the happiness is soon overshadowed by other news from Venice. This arrival also brings a complete change of direction; now there is a much greater involvement of Belmont in the affairs of Venice.

Bassanio describes to Portia the debt he owes Antonio and the trouble his friend is now in. The suggestions made in previous scenes that Antonio's ships might be at risk have come true. All his ventures have failed. Worse news is related by Salerio.

Shylock has demanded <u>justice</u>. He will not have repayment of the money due to him. As Antonio has not paid on time, Shylock is demanding payment of the forfeit. He demands justice and his bond: 'he would rather have Antonio's flesh / Than twenty times the value of the sum / That he [Antonio] did owe him.'
The realities of Shylock's plotting and desires are now disclosed. All his fine words, which Bassanio saw through, are now shown for what they really were: a ploy to get Antonio within his grasp.

> **❝** *Oh love! Dispatch all business and be gone!* **❞**

Portia swiftly supports Bassanio's desire to help his friend by placing all her wealth at his disposal, and suggests he depart for Venice as soon as they are married. <u>Her love for Bassanio knows no limits in what she is prepared to do for him</u>.

Similarly, Antonio's letter shows generosity of spirit to Bassanio. His only wish is that he should see Bassanio before his (Antonio's) death. Note that Bassanio's friendship for Antonio is equally generous in spirit.

He may have taken financial advantage of his more prosperous friends, but if you read the speech beginning 'O sweet Portia', you will understand the depth of his regard for Antonio and appreciate his honesty about himself.

Act 3, Scene 3

❝*Gaoler, look to him. Tell me not of mercy.*❞

This scene focuses on mercy. Ironically, <u>Shylock's determination to have nothing to do with mercy</u> will be at the root of his downfall. He sets his mind against it here, and continues to do so at the trial, concentrating instead on his bond and justice. He senses that he has Antonio at his mercy at last, but there is no mercy for Antonio in Shylock's heart.

Antonio recognises that the Duke of Venice cannot deny the course of law. To do so would destroy the credibility of Venice as a trading state. Antonio's only concern now is to see Bassanio so that he might 'see me pay his debt'. Antonio will willingly sacrifice his life for his friend. Contrast this with Shylock's repeated 'I'll have my bond'.

Act 3, Scene 4

❝*I never did repent for doing good*❞

Portia's intelligence and independence of thought, plus her keen moral sense, have been apparent before, but she has not been able to take a particularly active role. This now changes totally. She never repents doing good, and that now means taking risks and practising deceptions. <u>Portia reveals many different sides to her character here</u>. Her first speech expresses her spiritual view of human nature and society, none the less genuine for the deception about her intentions. Nothing could be more business-like than her instructions to Balthasar. Then suddenly she reveals a youthful sense of fun and adventure with Nerissa, boasting about what a fine-looking man she will be, parodying the speech and movement of youths in the transition to manhood, and even allowing herself a few 'lewd' jokes.

<u>Portia and Nerissa are in a long tradition of Shakespearean women who dress as men</u>. As boys played female parts in the Elizabethan theatre, the disguises were almost certainly more convincing than in many modern productions.

Act 3, Scene 5

> ❝ *Yes, truly; for, look you, the sins of the father are to be laid upon the children* ❞

The topic of Jessica's parentage, whether being Shylock's daughter dooms her to damnation, surfaces in a series of jokes from Launcelot. Many of these seem offensively prejudiced: consider 'I think you are damn'd' and the 'bastard hope' he finds for her. However, the offence is filtered through the sunny atmosphere of Belmont and Launcelot's known reputation as 'a wit-snapper'.

<u>The dialogue between Lorenzo and Jessica deals with ideals in love</u>. Jessica praises Portia as possessing heavenly qualities and surpassing all other women on Earth. Lorenzo's humorous boast in reply is not entirely flippant. All of the three Acts so far have switched the action between Venice and Belmont. Now we move from the lightness of this conversation to the drama of Act 4, which all takes place in Venice. When we return to spend Act 5 in Belmont, Jessica and Lorenzo's mood is unchanged in its serenity, with the beautiful 'In such a night' dialogue.

Uncover the plot

Delete two of the three alternatives given to find the correct plot. Beware possible misconceptions and muddles.

On the Rialto, Antonio's/Bassanio's/Tubal's ship is reported wrecked: Shylock hears the 'good news' from Salerio/Solanio/Tubal and resolves to 'have another bad match'/'have the heart of him'/'have hands, organs, dimensions, senses'. In Belmont, Bassanio chooses the gold/silver/lead casket, and wins Portia – while Gratiano/Lorenzo/Salerio declares his love for Nerissa. Salerio appears with a letter from Antonio/Shylock/the Duke. Portia offers to pay 3,000/6,000/36,000 ducats to cancel Antonio's bond and sends Bassanio to his friend — meanwhile planning to 'live in prayer and contemplation'/go disguised to Venice/'pay the petty debt 20 times over'. In Venice, Antonio resigns himself to death, if he can only have revenge on Shylock/pay back his debt/see Bassanio once more. Left in Belmont, Jessica and Launcelot/the Duke/Lorenzo start their life together.

Who? What? Where? When? Why?

1   Who are the 'Jasons', and what 'fleece' have they won?

2   Who is given the 'husbandry and manage' of Portia's house?

3   Who is it 'in whom / The ancient Roman honour more appears / Than any that draws breath in Italy'?

4   What does Portia 'give ... with this ring'?

5   What are more different than jet and ivory?

6   What is Shylock's 'loss upon loss'?

7   Where are Nerissa and Portia supposed to await their husbands' return?

8   Who is Portia's cousin, where does he live, and what does she ask him for?

9   Why is Portia inclined to delay the choice of caskets?

10   Why does Antonio think Shylock hates him?

Act 4

Act 4, Scene 1

> ❝*Make room and let him stand before our face.*❞

The play has changed pace: both Act 4 and Act 5 consist of one formally arranged scene (with, in Act 4, one tiny extra scene which follows on immediately). You need to be aware of the formal pattern of the trial scene. It's relentless logic is brought out by the repetitions and the formal offers and decisions.

The whole scene is a demonstration of the need for mercy. Observe how mercy runs through the scene like a refrain: the first reference is in line 6 and you will be able to find many more. When Portia says, 'Then must the Jew be merciful', she is not saying that he must in law, but that this is the only course of action available morally.

Shylock, of course, takes the other option: the law and the bond. These phrases also echo throughout the scene. Portia gives him a chance to observe the spirit rather than the letter of the bond (the surgeon) but it is Shylock's choice that the exact letter be observed. The resulting irony is that, when Portia says 'The Jew shall have all justice', Shylock receives just what he has insisted on — justice without mercy.

Look at how Bassanio and Gratiano fall into the trap of placing the love of Antonio above the love of their wives. Is it inevitable that they will fail the ring bond test? The situation is unfairly set up against them, but this is a formal lesson in honour and a formal progression towards responsibility and mercy.

The Duke's greeting for Antonio is warm, but he damns Shylock with great forcefulness, calling him 'A stony adversary, an inhuman wretch, / Uncapable of pity, void and empty / From any dram of mercy.' The Duke is hardly, in modern eyes, a suitable judge. However, Shylock has already lost our pity and the Duke's words merely serve to confirm the audience's views.

Antonio tells the Duke that he accepts the verdict of the law and will oppose Shylock's fury with patience and a 'quietness of spirit'. This points to his noble nature, already demonstrated in the sacrifices he has made for Bassanio and voiced in the letter where his last wish was to see Bassanio before dying.

Notwithstanding his jaundiced view of Shylock, the Duke tries to reason with him, and attempts to play upon feelings of compassion and mercy for a fellow human being. This is an interesting parallel with Shylock's own 'If you prick us' speech. There, Shylock tried to gain our sympathy for his cause by appealing to the common fellowship and feelings of man. Here, the Duke tries a similar plea, but it falls on deaf ears.

Explore

Why do you think that Shylock is in this mood, apparently quite relaxed, even humorous in his account of people who cannot tolerate the 'harmless necessary cat' or those in whom bagpipes provoke incontinence?

The import of Shylock's long response to the Duke is that he would rather have the pound of flesh than the money because it 'humours' him, and the only reason he can give is a 'lodged hate and a certain loathing' he has for Antonio. These comparatively weak responses contrast strongly with the virulence of the hatred and desire for revenge he has previously expressed for Antonio.

Antonio joins this discussion by stating plainly that he knows Shylock will not forgo his rights to the forfeit. Antonio recognises and accepts the inevitability of the law's judgement and the implacable determination of Shylock to pursue his legal case. He accuses Shylock of having a hard heart — and therefore no capacity for friendship, love or mercy.

When Bassanio offers him yet more money, Shylock refuses. He says that even if the 6,000 ducats offered were multiplied by six (i.e. 36,000) he would 'not draw them'. It is interesting that, without knowing it, he has here rejected the very amount that Portia said she would be willing to pay. By implication he is already rejecting her, just as he will reject her plea for mercy.

> **How shalt thou hope for mercy, rend'ring none?**

Explore

Do be aware that Elizabethan views regarding slavery do not sit easily with twenty-first century attitudes.

The Duke's question prepares us for the time when the court and its officers will show Shylock no mercy. Shylock here effectively <u>seals his own fate</u> by rejecting mercy and desiring only the law. His accusation, in his own defence, that the Venetians treat their slaves without compassion, regarding them as property to do with as they will, perhaps makes us a little uneasy.

Before Portia, disguised as a young lawyer, makes her appearance, Bassanio <u>offers to lay down his own life for Antonio</u>, a sacrifice as great as Antonio is prepared to make for him. Antonio is very passive throughout this scene: others try to save him, while he accepts his fate. His speeches emphasise the uselessness of reasoning with Shylock. Is it simply his 'quietness of spirit', which he mentions at the beginning, or is there an element of despair, both at his fate and at himself?

Following hard on the heels of Antonio's and Bassanio's eloquent willingness to die for each other, we have the almost obscene picture of <u>Shylock whetting (sharpening) his knife</u>, ready and anxious to cut into Antonio's flesh. The intervention of Gratiano who, in typically robust fashion, roundly curses Shylock and accuses him of being 'wolvish, bloody, starved and ravenous', provides a short respite, allowing Portia, disguised as Balthasar, a young lawyer from Padua, to be introduced.

> **❝*Then must the Jew be merciful.*❞**

Once the brief formalities of identifying Shylock and Antonio, and of confirming their acknowledgement of the bond are over, Portia confirms the rule of Venetian law and declares that for Antonio to escape death, the Jew must be merciful. Note how this immediately echoes the Duke's earlier pleas to Shylock. We are, of course, already aware of Shylock's response to the Duke on this count, and are not surprised when Shylock asks under what compulsion he must be merciful.

> **❝*The quality of mercy is not strain'd*❞**

Perhaps the most famous of the speeches from this play, <u>Portia's powerful exposition of the quality of and reason for mercy</u> makes little impression on Shylock. The speech is intense and compressed. It operates in paired ideas: mercy blesses twice (the giver and the taker); mercy is mightier than the power of kings' 'sceptred sway', but it lives in the 'heart of kings'; it is 'an attribute to God himself' and can make Earthly power resemble God's; our seeking mercy (from God) teaches us mercy (towards our fellow humans).

> **❝*mercy seasons justice*❞**

Justice is what Shylock demands. <u>Portia shows that justice will bring none of us to salvation unless we also have mercy</u>. However, she concludes that if Shylock rejects the plea for mercy then this 'strict court of Venice' must give judgement against Antonio, the merchant of Venice.

When Bassanio pleads with her to bend the laws of Venice: <u>'To do a great right, do a little wrong'</u>, she pointedly refuses because of the precedents such an action would set, which might then lead to even greater wrongs being done in the future. Her response is greeted with glee by Shylock and he charges her 'by the law' to proceed to judgement.

It is at this point that <u>Portia encourages Shylock to show everyone how far he is prepared to go</u>, and the true inhumanity and lack of mercy which accompany the deed. Shylock will use his own knife, sharpened in full view of the

audience, and will cut the flesh himself. He has brought his own set of scales to weigh the flesh, and is scornful of Portia when she suggests that for humanity's sake he should provide a surgeon to stop the bleeding: 'Is it so nominated in the bond?' He will have his bond, and nothing else.

For a brief moment, Antonio and Bassanio reaffirm their love and friendship for each other in a dignified and touching scene, particularly in contrast to the bloodthirsty attitude of Shylock.

The audience is reminded of the true relationships between the characters at this point, when both Portia and Nerissa react to Bassanio and Gratiano's declarations that they are prepared to sacrifice their own lives, together with their wives, to free Antonio. This also prepares us for the moment when the disguised Portia and Nerissa want to obtain the rings they gave their husbands. By then, they want 'revenge' for these words and for the breaking of the ring bond.

❝The law allows it and the court awards it❞

<u>This is the moment of triumph for Shylock</u>. All his dreams have come true. He has gained justice according to his bond, and soon his enemy will lie dead. Revenge will be sweet and, presumably, profit even sweeter. But his happiness does not last

Explore

Be aware of the tension in this scene as Shakespeare takes the audience closer and closer to Antonio's death.

long, for Portia intervenes just as he is about to cut Antonio's flesh. The very law by which he hoped to gain his aims will prove to be his downfall.

Shylock, however, is not only frustrated in his desire to gain revenge. He also suffers at the hands of the law. And one begins to get the uncomfortable feeling that perhaps

this time it is Portia and the Christians of Venice who will exact revenge and not temper their justice with mercy. If, the law proclaims, he takes even the merest too much or too little of Antonio's flesh and spills even a drop of Antonio's blood, then he loses his goods and his life. Naturally, he declines and prepares to depart with nothing. However, the law has yet another hold on him. As he, a foreigner, conspired to take the life of a Venetian, half his goods must go to Antonio, half to the state of Venice, and his life is at the Duke's mercy.

Given the extreme penalties that the court could exact from Shylock, perhaps the 'quality of mercy' is demonstrated by the Duke and Antonio. The Duke does not have him executed and Antonio intercedes on his behalf so that the court may 'quit the fine for one half of his goods'. He will use the other and, on Shylock's death, will give it to Lorenzo, Jessica's husband, to whom will pass every other part of Shylock's wealth.

Perhaps the crowning fate is Antonio's demand that Shylock should become a Christian. Is this really mercy? Can it be justified? Elizabethans may well have seen this as comic retribution to mete out to a non-Christian. There is appropriateness, if not mercy, in the punishment, given Shylock's well-known hatred of Christians. We can, at least, feel that the Christians, despite the smugness that besets them throughout the play, have been more merciful than Shylock intended to be and have made one stipulation founded on charity: the gift to Jessica and Lorenzo.

> **And, for your love,
> I'll take this ring from you.**

Anxious to reward the lawyer, Bassanio tries to persuade 'him' to accept the ducats which Shylock turned down. Portia refuses but, when pressed, wickedly demands the ring she had given him. It is only after Bassanio has been persuaded by Antonio that he reluctantly accedes to her demand.

By the end of this long scene, the play's central bond has been resolved and the major themes of 'love and friendship versus greed' and 'mercy versus justice' played out.

Act 4, Scene 2

> **we'll outface them, and outswear them too**

This short, final scene of Act 4 sees the resolution of the ring plot. This re-establishes the action as comedy.

The Merchant of Venice is not a typical <u>Shakespearean</u> <u>comedy</u>. For example, it nearly becomes the tragedy of Antonio, and some productions have tried to turn it into the tragedy of Shylock. However, the nature of Shakespearean comedy is <u>not</u> <u>simply</u> <u>a</u> <u>matter</u> <u>of</u> <u>humour.</u> It has to do with <u>a</u> <u>resolution</u> <u>that</u> <u>is</u> <u>both</u> <u>happy</u> <u>and</u> <u>morally</u> <u>satisfying</u>, as supplied in Belmont in Act 5. It concerns a balance of principal characters, with the emphasis on themes (perhaps self-knowledge or mercy) and a certain view of the world as much as on individuals. Shakespearean comedy also tends to develop its plots via disguises and misunderstandings which often reveal genuine aspects of character.

Uncover the plot

Delete two of the three alternatives given to find the correct plot. Beware possible misconceptions and muddles.

Before the court, Shylock is adamant in his demand for three thousand ducats/six thousand ducats/the pound of flesh. Bassanio/Balthasar/Bellario tries to encourage Antonio. Portia appears as the lawyer Bellario/Balthasar/Belmont and after an appeal for justice/the law/mercy, judges that the law is on Antonio's/Shylock's/the Duke's side: the bond must be fulfilled. But there is a catch: since it is not in the bond, Shylock cannot cut the flesh from Antonio's breast/have a surgeon standing by/shed blood. The penalty would be his land and goods/half his land and goods/his life. Bound by the justice he has demanded, Shylock offers to take 3,000/9,000/36,000 ducats, but — charged with usury/treason/attempted murder of a Venetian — he escapes with his life only through the mercy of the Duke/Antonio/Portia. Portia persuades Bassanio to give her his gloves/purse/ring in thanks. The friends all depart for Padua/Belmont/Venice.

Who? What? Where? When? Why?

1   Whom does Shylock call a 'noble judge' and 'excellent young man'?

2   What does Shylock refuse to do because it is not in the bond?

3   What is the penalty for an attempt on the life of a Venetian citizen by an alien?

4   What three penalties are finally imposed on Shylock?

5   What do Bassanio and Antonio offer 'Balthasar' for 'his' services — and what does he accept?

6   When has Shylock sworn 'to have the due and forfeit of my bond'?

7   When does 'earthly power show likest God's'?

8   Why is mercy 'twice blest'?

9   Why will 'Balthasar' not 'do a great right, do a little wrong'?

10   Why will 'the deed' to be signed by Shylock be 'welcome to Lorenzo'?

Act 5

Act 5 Scene 1

The scene returns to Belmont. The trial is over and Antonio is safe. Shylock is defeated, and soon the various parties will return. Lorenzo and Jessica, conjuring up classical images and relaxing in the moonlight, present a scene of peace and happiness only slightly marred by references to 'the wealthy Jew'. But their love for each other and the influence of Belmont is unmistakable, a vivid contrast to the drama of the previous scene.

Explore

Consider what the importance of Lorenzo and Jessica, uninvolved in the recent dramas, is in this scene.

The formality of the opening, with the repeated 'In such a night', emphasises the poetry and Classical artifice of the lines. Lorenzo and Jessica (and by implication the other lovers) are linked to such famed couples as Pyramus and Thisbe and Troilus and Cressida, before both relax into affectionate banter.

News is brought that Portia is to return, as will Bassanio. Look at the images presented in Lorenzo's two speeches, 'Sweet soul, let's in' and 'The reason is your spirits are attentive'. His praise of music and the harmony it brings encapsulates the spirit of Belmont and its inhabitants. Note the words 'The man that hath no music in himself ... Is fit for treasons, stratagems'. Shakespeare has very definite views about man and music. In *Much Ado About Nothing* he likens human love to music, 'the true concord of human sound'. In *Julius Caesar*, Caesar observes of Cassius: 'he hears no music ... such men ... are very dangerous'.

"By yonder moon I swear you do me wrong!"

Explore

See what other references to light and dark you can find. Here, the choice of the changeable moon to swear by is perhaps an unwise choice.

As well as music, imagery of light is very important in this scene: the moonlight and the distant candle in the house help to create a mood of serenity and romance. The combination of moonlight and music in 'How sweet the moonlight sleeps upon this bank' is a strikingly beautiful appeal to the senses. But there are many references to light which have specific meanings, notably Portia's reference to the candle: 'So shines a good deed in a naughty world.'

It is a mistake to see the argument between Portia and Nerissa and their hapless husbands as being no more than teasing. Of course the women know the circumstances and how the men were placed in a difficult position; of course they intend no long-term punishment or serious row. However, a constant element in Shakespearean comedy is the testing of characters in situations which appear to be real. Bassanio and Gratiano have failed this test and need to be made to squirm before it is all revealed as an illusion. Note the formal solemnity of Bassanio's and Portia's speeches, with each line ending in 'the ring'. The point being made is that, though Antonio's life had to be saved, now Bassanio must put aside the habits of a bachelor: now the bond that matters is with Portia.

Events, however, come full circle when Antonio intervenes and again offers to enter into a bond for his friend Bassanio, 'I dare be bound again, / My soul upon the forfeit, that your lord / Will never more break faith advisedly.' The forfeit this time, Antonio's soul, is rather more than a pound of flesh. However, in the world of love, friendship and Belmont, there can be no doubt that Antonio will never be called upon to pay the forfeit.

Text commentary

Portia delivers a letter which reveals that she and Nerissa were the doctor (lawyer) and clerk. She also delivers news that three of Antonio's ships have safely docked and that his fortune is therefore safe. To Jessica and Lorenzo she delivers news of how they shall inherit all of Shylock's wealth when he dies.

Not much is made of the news of <u>Antonio's</u> <u>escape</u> <u>from</u> <u>bankruptcy</u>, though admittedly he is struck dumb with delight. Shakespeare does not even bother to make the news particularly convincing. Portia just knows it, having come across a letter by 'strange accident'. In Act 3 such an event would have transformed the plot. Shakespeare's <u>offhand</u> <u>treatment</u> of this derives from the fact that the missing argosies were another artifice to present the characters with a moral test: one which only Shylock completely failed.

Explore

Consider how Shakespeare chooses to close the play. Why is this? Would the trial not have made a more dramatic ending?

In a typical ending for a Shakespearean comedy, <u>lovers</u> <u>are</u> <u>united</u> after their happiness has been threatened on various fronts. What is unusual in this play is the form the threats have taken, with the comedy nearly overbalanced by the character and situation of Shylock. Note, though, what is stressed in Gratiano's closing lines (in rhyming couplets, for greater emphasis): 'Well, while I live I'll fear no other thing / So sore as keeping safe Nerissa's ring.'

Uncover the plot

Delete two of the three alternatives given to find the correct plot. Beware possible misconceptions and muddles.

In Belmont, Lorenzo and Jessica/Cressida/Nerissa spend the night talking, when Stephano/Solanio/Salerio enters to announce Portia's return, and Launcelot to announce Antonio's/Bassanio's/Gratiano's. In a brief interlude, Lorenzo talks of the 'sweet power' of moonlight/stillness/music. Portia/Nerissa/Jessica starts a mock argument with Gratiano about his late arrival/vehement oaths/missing ring. Bassanio is drawn in, until Antonio backs him up again — this time with his soul/body/fortune. Portia reveals herself as Bellario/the clerk/the doctor, and with more good news for Lorenzo and Gratiano/Antonio/Shylock, the play ends.

Who? What? Where? When? Why?

1   'To whom', 'for whom' and 'for what' did Bassanio give the ring?

2   Who is called 'a kind of boy' — and why is this a joke?

3   What 'becomes the touches of sweet harmony'?

4   Where does the scene take place?

5   Why is Antonio 'th' unhappy subject of these quarrels'?

Who said that?

1   Who says: 'Such harmony is in immortal souls'?

2   Who says: 'Sweet lady, you have given me life and living', to whom and why?

3   Who says: 'By heaven, I will ne'er come in your bed/Until I see the ring', and why is this a joke?

Writing essays on *The Merchant of Venice*

- The first essential requirement is thorough revision. You will have time to look up quotations and references, but only if you know where to look.

- Read the questions carefully, making sure you underline key words that tell you what to do, e.g 'compare', 'contrast', 'explore', 'explain'. Retelling the story will get you no credit.

- Jot down the main points, **make an essay plan** that shows what you are going to include in each paragraph, then stick to it (see page 66). Make sure you link the paragraphs to each other and refer back to the question so as not to digress.

- Summarise in your introduction how you plan to approach the question, then jump straight into your argument. Ensure you answer *all* of the question, not just part of it.

- Take care with spelling, punctuation and grammar. Avoid using slang or abbreviations. Write in paragraphs, starting a new line and indenting quotations of more than a few words. Quotations should be used to increase the clarity of your answer, but extended quotations (more than a few sentences) are usually unhelpful.

- It is important to back up what you say. Remember: **point–quotation–comment** (see page 62). This will ensure that your work stays analytical.

- Finally, use your conclusion to sum up your points and relate them back to the question. If you have missed something, put it in now. Leave five minutes to proofread your work for mistakes.

- Most of you will write a coursework essay on *The Merchant of Venice* fulfilling the Shakespeare requirement for English and English Literature. In order to meet the requirements it will be necessary to fulfil the following criteria:

  - You must show awareness of the historical and social context. In this play Elizabethan anti-Semitism is extremely important, as is knowledge of Venice as a trading nation.

  - You should develop an argument, avoiding becoming too narrative. Make an essay plan and stick to it (see page 66). Refer back to the question while writing the essay to avoid digressing. When writing a comparative piece, the comparison should be made throughout the essay not just at the end.

- Take advantage of being able to draft your essay so that the neat copy is as polished as possible.

- As with examination essays, quote from the text to support your points and make sure your conclusion summarises your arguments. Only at this stage can you consider giving your opinion. The main body of the essay should not contain personal pronouns. Again, don't forget to proofread.

- Essays will generally be expected to be 1000–1500 words in length, but follow the advice of your teacher.

- You can display your knowledge of text through one or more of the following ways:
  scene analysis
  character study
  analysis of imagery or other linguistic features
  dramatic effect of the play/one or two key scenes
  reflections on a production.

Writing essays

Key quotations

The following are examples of **points, quotations** and **comments** that could be used in an essay on *The Merchant of Venice*.

1 Shylock informs the audience in an aside about the reasons for his hatred towards Antonio:

> " *I hate him for he is a Christian;*
> *But more, for that in low simplicity*
> *He lends out money gratis, and brings down*
> *The rate of usance here with us in Venice.* "
> *(Act 1, Scene 3)*

This demonstrates that Shylock despises Antonio both for his religion and because his money-lending affects Shylock's livelihood. Christians were not allowed to charge interest on loans and therefore, as they were not constrained by this, many Jews made their living from usury. Antonio, by lending money for nothing, is preventing Shylock from earning more.

2 Shylock pleads for understanding in what is ultimately the most sympathetic speech in the play:

> " *I am a Jew. Hath not a Jew eyes? Hath not a Jew*
> *hands, organs, dimensions, senses, affections,*
> *passions?* " *(Act 3, Scene 1)*

He asks for understanding and gives the audience some indication of his anger at the way he is treated by the Christian community. He explains that, like a Christian would, he will have his revenge when wronged.

3 Portia demonstrates her love for Bassanio when, shortly after their exchange of rings, he receives news that Antonio needs him in Venice.

> *"O love! Dispatch all business and be gone."*
> *(Act 3, Scene 2)*

It is to Portia's credit that she is willing to allow Bassanio to leave so soon after he has 'won' her. She realises the importance of his friendship with Antonio and wants to help in any way she can.

4 Portia disguises herself as a Doctor of Law and tries to persuade Shylock to show mercy to Antonio rather than demanding the strict letter of the law:

> *"The quality of mercy is not strain'd [...]*
> *It is twice blest: / It blesseth him that gives, and him*
> *that takes."* *(Act 4, Scene 4)*

This demonstrates the importance of being merciful to others and is the beginning of a long speech to this effect. It seems ironic, then, that in dispensing the letter of the law Portia later shows no mercy to Shylock.

1. Discuss the impact of the trial scene. You should discuss its effect as a drama, the ways in which it reveals character, its examination of the main themes of the play and its place in the effectiveness of the play as a whole.

2. Examine the presentation of various forms of love in The Merchant of Venice. Identify what the characteristics of each are and show how they change or develop during the play.

3. 'The best condition'd and unwearied spirit / In doing courtesies.' 'I am a tainted wether of the flock.' Which seems to you to be the more accurate decription of Antonio's character? You should consider his words and deeds throughout the play and also the opinions others hold of him.

4. To what extent does Portia fulfil the image of fairy-tale princess?

5. Shylock is the archetypal villain of the piece. Discuss.

6. To what extent do you believe that The Merchant of Venice can accurately be described as a comedy?

7. Explore the theme of disguise in the play. What effect does the use of disguise have on the female characters?

8. To what degree do you think it could be said that justice is served by the end of the play?

9. Venice is a place of finance and Belmont is a place of love. Assess to what extent this is true.

10. Women in Shakespeare are only empowered when disguised as men. Is this true in The Merchant of Venice?

11. The play can be seen as a series of tests of the characters' morality. How far could this be seen to be true?

12. None of the characters in The Merchant of Venice are truly moral. Discuss this statement with close reference to the text.

13. Discuss to what degree Shylock's behaviour merely reflects that of his Christian persecutors.

14. Why do you think the play is entitled The Merchant of Venice?

15. How do the bonds made in this play reflect the characters of those involved?

16. Discuss the view that Bassanio is nothing more than a wastrel and a spendthrift.

17. In The Merchant of Venice, is justice or mercy more important?

18. Explore the view that The Merchant of Venice shows Shakespeare to be anti-Semitic.

19. Explore the different types of prejudice in the play.

20. Compare and contrast the characters of Antonio and Shylock in the play.

Spidergram essay plans for questions 1, 5 and 9 are given on pages 67–69.

There are several ways of planning an essay either for coursework or as part of an examination. One of the quickest, simplest and easiest to follow is the spidergram. Creating a spidergram is easy, just complete the following steps.

- Put the key words of the essay question in the centre of your map and work outwards from this.

- Make sure you use different colours if the essay asks you to look at either different characters or different themes. This will make them easy to isolate at a glance.

- Draw lines out from the centre that relate directly to the question. From these lines, draw further lines and write anything specifically related to this area of the question.

- Remember, only have one idea at the end of each line or your drawing may become confusing.

- The next few pages show you how you could use spidergrams to plan the answers to three of the sample essay questions.

If you find that using spidergrams is not for you, don't panic, there are other ways of planning your answers.

- You can underline the key words in the title to ensure that you understand the focus of the essay.

- Then write down in bullet points what will be included in each paragraph from the introduction to the conclusion.

- Next, try to find relevant quotations to support your points and either write down the quotation or page reference so that it can be easily found.

Ensure that you stick to your plan and refer back to the question so as not to digress from it.

In an examination, always hand in any plan that you have written as you may be given some credit for it if you are unable to complete the full essay.

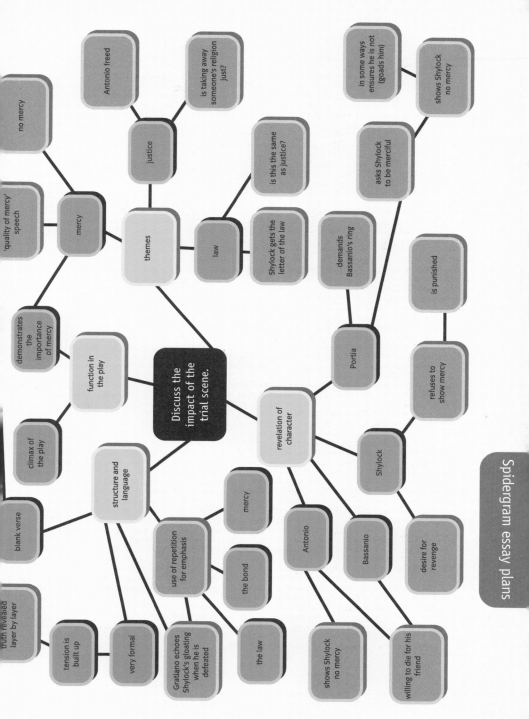

Discuss the impact of the trial scene.

themes
- justice
  - Antonio freed
  - is taking away someone's religion just?
- mercy
  - 'quality of mercy' speech
  - no mercy
- law
  - is this the same as justice?
  - Shylock gets the letter of the law

function in the play
- demonstrates the importance of mercy
- climax of the play

structure and language
- blank verse
- truth revealed layer by layer
- tension is built up
- very formal
- Gratiano echoes Shylock's gloating when he is defeated
- use of repetition for emphasis
  - mercy
  - the bond
  - the law

revelation of character
- Portia
  - asks Shylock to be merciful
    - in some ways ensures he is not (goads him)
    - shows Shylock no mercy
  - demands Bassanio's ring
  - is punished
  - refuses to show mercy
- Shylock
  - desire for revenge
- Bassanio
- Antonio
  - shows Shylock no mercy
  - willing to die for his friend

Shylock is the archetypal villain of the piece. Discuss.

sympathetic *villain*

- betrayed by his daughter
  - she steals his money and the ring his wife gave him
  - she elopes with a Christian
  - she has no respect for her ancestry
- racially taunted by Christians
  - speech asking for tolerance: 'I am a Jew...'
  - Antonio claims he will continue to spit on Shylock

Shakespeare's intentions
- 'human'
- comic villain
  - amusing scene about ducats and daughter
  - despised by English

historical background
- Jews banned from England until mid-17th century
- mistreated worldwide

villain
- treatment of Jessica and Launcelot
- creating the bond in the first place
- attitude to Jessica eloping
- even sympathy speech shows desire for revenge
- gloats when he thinks he has won
- refusal to show mercy
  - desire to murder Antonio
  - demands the letter of the law

audina

wants revenge
- Antonio
- Christians
- daughter

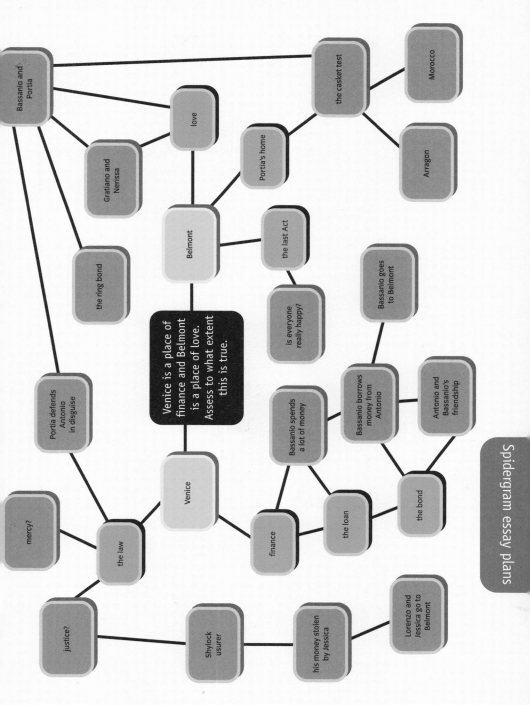

Venice is a place of finance and Belmont is a place of love. Assess to what extent this is true.

- Bassanio and Portia
- the casket test
- Morocco
- Arragon
- love
- Portia's home
- Gratiano and Nerissa
- Belmont
- the last Act
- the ring bond
- is everyone really happy?
- Bassanio goes to Belmont
- Portia defends Antonio in disguise
- Bassanio spends a lot of money
- Bassanio borrows money from Antonio
- Antonio and Bassanio's friendship
- Venice
- the bond
- mercy?
- the law
- finance
- the loan
- justice?
- Shylock usurer
- his money stolen by Jessica
- Lorenzo and Jessica go to Belmont

Spidergram essay plans

69

Sample response

Shylock is the archetypal villain of the piece. Discuss.

Shylock is one of Shakespeare's most famous characters and is widely seen to be a villain. Certainly an Elizabethan audience would have expected him to be and would have wanted to see him punished at the end of the play. ✓ Audiences years later have seen how you could feel sorry for Shylock but he is left with nothing by the end of the play, which is a sign that Shakespeare did not want him to be sympathised with too much. ✓ He is based on Barabas, the main character in Marlowe's 'Jew of Malta', a play about an evil Jew. It is possible to see Shylock in this light.

From the very beginning he shows his prejudice towards Christians. When Antonio comes to borrow money from him he calculatedly works out how best to entrap him. ✓ He says that if Antonio cannot repay the money he owes then

'let the forfeit
Be nominated for an equal pound
Of your fair flesh, to be cut off and taken
In what part of your body pleaseth me.'

This shows that Shylock is not only willing but determined to kill Antonio if he cannot repay the debt. He is shown to be a villain who wants the death of a man who hates him and treats him very badly. ✓ He is shown to hate Antonio both as a Christian and as a moneylender. ✓ Shylock himself is a moneylender and would charge people who borrowed money interest on their debts. Antonio, as a Christian, is not allowed to charge interest and lends out money for free. This stops Shylock earning as much. Even when he relates his speech about being a Jew, revenge is at the forefront of his mind. ✓ He says

'If you prick us do we not bleed [...]
And if you wrong us, shall we not revenge?'

He asks for understanding but then makes it clear that all he wants is revenge.✓ His daughter has eloped with a Christian and he is furious as she stole his money and some of his possessions. ✓ He says he wants to see her dead and makes it obvious that he is more upset about his money than anything else. ✓ He hears from Tubal how much she managed to spend:

'Thou stick'st a dagger in me; I shall never see my gold again. Four score ducats at a sitting! Four score ducats!'

This shows what a miser he is, how money is really the only thing that matters to him. Again, he is shown to have qualities you would expect from a villain. ✓

When the trial takes place he will not show mercy to Antonio and demands his pound of flesh. He wants to cut it himself in front of the court. He will not even accept more money than he is owed. ✓ He says:

'I crave the law,
The penalty and forfeit of my bond.'
He is single-minded in his intent, he wants Antonio's life and

nothing else. He is unwilling to show mercy and therefore is shown none himself by Portia, Antonio and the court. Shylock is punished as the villain he is and the Elizabethan audience would have wanted him to be. ✓

Although Shylock is treated badly by the Christians in the play and his daughter elopes with one and takes his money with her, he is still the villain. It is he who wants the life of Antonio and will not show mercy. ✓ Shakespeare punishes Shylock for his evil behaviour and leaves him with nothing. He is faced with a moral test and fails it, he refuses to allow Antonio to be freed. ✓ He fails to show human compassion and thus proves his villainy. ✓ Perhaps he is not an archetypal villain as he does have a few human qualities, but ultimately the audience is supposed to hate him and be glad that good triumphs over evil. ✓

Examiner's comments

This essay uses the text well to express the villainy of Shylock and demonstrates a clear understanding of the play. However, it is not really detailed enough and the candidate needed to focus on the 'human' side of Shylock in more than just the conclusion. Also, avoid using personal pronouns in a formal essay except in the conclusion.

Sample response

Shylock is the archetypal villain of the piece. Discuss.

In Shakespearean England anti-Semitism was rife. Jews were widely regarded as evil and the entire community had been expelled from England in 1290. ✓ They were not allowed to return until the mid-seventeenth century and therefore, in Shakespeare's time, there were no Jews in England. Jews were persecuted worldwide and it is fair to assume that an Elizabethan audience would have wanted the Jewish character to be a villain and ultimately to be punished for his actions. ✓

The character of Shylock was based in part on Christopher Marlowe's Jew of Malta, who was named Barabas, after the man who was freed at the cruxifiction instead of Jesus. Barabas was a villainous character and it could be argued that Shylock is the same. He is a usurer and hates the Christian community. ✓ In the first scene he appears in he says in an aside to the audience:

'I hate him for he is a Christian;
But more, for that in low simplicity
He lends out money gratis, and brings down
The rate of usance here with us in Venice.'

This demonstrates that his reasons for hating Antonio are not only his religion and treatment of Jews, but the fact that he lends money to people without charging interest and thus adversely affects Shylock's livelihood. ✓ This open demonstration of his greed and hatred makes Shylock immediately seem an unsympathetic character. ✓ This view of him as self-serving and avaracious is compounded by his reaction to his daughter eloping with a Christian. He is outraged that she has left and has stolen his money. He exclaims: 'I would my daughter were dead at my foot.'

Again Shylock shows himself in an unfavourable light, as vindictive and villainous. He wishes for the death of his own daughter as the price for her treachery and even goes so far as to wish that the ducats were in the coffin with her dead body as evidence of what she has done. This shows Shylock to be a cold, heartless man, utterly devoid of parental feeling, whose mind is focused purely on revenge and money. ✓

He is unable to avenge himself upon Jessica, but receives the opportunity to make the Christians suffer through Antonio instead. ✓ This, coupled with his hatred for Antonio as an individual, provides the perfect opportunity for retribution. Antonio's ships sink and thus he cannot repay the bond he owes Shylock. Shylock is determined that Antonio must abide by their agreed bond, one which would ultimately result in Antonio's death. ✓ The pound of flesh bond is utterly inhumane, yet despite various pleas for mercy, Shylock is determined to have what he is entitled to by law. ✓ He sits slavering over his knife, fully intending to cut the flesh himself in the open courtroom, refusing even to allow a surgeon to be present. 'Is it so nominated in the bond?'

He shows himself to be a cruel, heartless murderer who is totally incapable of showing mercy and, in this way, he could easily be perceived to be an archetypal villain. ✓ His punishment at the end of the play, losing his wealth, property and being forced to become a Christian certainly suggest that this is the case. The villain is punished and the threat is over. ✓

However, if Shylock is indeed an 'archetypal' villain, why is he afforded the most sympathetic speech in the play? ✓

'I am a Jew. Hath not a Jew eyes? Hath not a Jew
hands, organs, dimensions, senses, affections, passions?'

Shylock tries to make the Christians and indeed the audience aware that he is human and has feelings, and that he has been severely mistreated by others. ✓

'The villainy you
teach me I will execute,'

It could be argued that he merely intends to treat the Christians the way they treat him, cursing him and spitting on his Jewish gaberdine. ✓ Furthermore, they are without remorse, Antonio admits he would readily do this again. Surely no one could blame Shylock for being enraged by such blatant racism. ✓

Moreover, his only daughter elopes with one of his Christian persecutors, steals his money and exchanges the ring his wife gave him for a monkey. It seems reasonable that he should feel betrayed. He only demands a bond that Antonio agreed to and it could be argued that if Antonio was unwilling to die he never should have consented to the conditions Shylock put forward. ✓

Throughout the eighteenth century he was perceived as a villain, through the nineteenth a victim and today's audiences have mixed feelings about Shylock. He becomes throughout the play, an increasingly isolated figure and is shown by Shakespeare to be in some ways very 'human'. ✓ He is given the most sympathetic speech in the play and his Christian persecutors are not always shown in a favourable light. He is betrayed by his daughter and is entitled to feel angry and hurt. However, ultimately he deliberately devises a bond that will result in a human being's death and is unwilling to show mercy. ✓ He is also a greedy miser who makes his daughter and his servant Launcelot Gobbo's lives a misery. It is Shakespeare's decision to leave Shylock utterly defeated at the end of the play, without so much as his religion to hold onto, that indicates that Shylock is intended to be seen to some extent as a villain. ✓ Regardless of this he is not an 'archetypal villain', he inspires too much empathy in an audience to ever be that. ✓

Examiner's comments

A very thorough essay that shows a clear understanding of both sides of the argument, and a good use of the text. The candidate could have explored the notion of Shylock as a comedy villain and looked more closely at the use of language.

Quick quiz answers

Quick quiz 1
Uncover the plot

Antonio is the Merchant of Venice. He <u>has money tied up in trade</u>, and goes to the moneylender <u>Shylock</u> to borrow <u>three thousand ducats</u> for his friend <u>Bassanio</u>. It is agreed that if the money is not repaid in <u>three months</u>, the forfeit will be '<u>an equal pound of your fair flesh</u>'.

Who? What? Where? When? Why?

1 County Palatine (Act 1, Scene 2)
2 Prince of Morocco (Act 1, Scene 2)
3 Antonio (Act 1, Scene 3)
4 Bassanio (Act 1, Scene 1)
5 Shylock; as the devil (Act 1, Scene 3)
6 Antonio; sadness (Act 1, Scene 1)
7 Falconbridge, Monsieur le Bon, County Palatine, etc. (Act 1, Scene 2)
8 the forfeit of a pound of flesh (Act 1, Scene 3)
9 the world (Act 1, Scene 1)
10 shoot an arrow in the same direction as the one lost, in order to find both (Act 1, Scene 1)

Open quotes

1 'My ventures are not in one bottom trusted, nor to one place.' (Act 1, Scene 1)
2 'To buy his favour, I extend this friendship.' (Act 1 Scene 3)
3 'I will feed fat the ancient grudge I bear him.' (Act 1, Scene 3)

Quick quiz 2
Uncover the plot

In <u>Belmont</u>, the casket bond proceeds: with two suitors already rejected, news comes that <u>Bassanio</u> is at Portia's gate. Meanwhile, Shylock is left bewailing the loss of '<u>my ducats and my daughter</u>'. His servant <u>Launcelot</u> has left him for Bassanio, and his daughter <u>Jessica</u> has eloped with Lorenzo — and the treasure. There is, however, some news that will gladden Shylock's heart: '<u>there miscarried / A vessel of our country richly fraught</u>'.

Who? What? Where? When? Why?

1 Launcelot (Act 2, Scene 5)
2 Gratiano; by Bassanio (Act 2, Scene 2)
3 boy's clothes; torch bearer (Act 2, Scene 4)
4 'Never to unfold to any one / Which casket 'twas I chose'; 'Never to speak to a lady afterward / In way of marriage'; 'Immediately to leave you and be gone' (Act 2, Scene 9)
5 justice, law, ducats, daughter, jewels (Act 2, Scene 8)
6 to search Bassanio's ship (with the Duke) (Act 2, Scene 8)
7 at dinner with Bassanio (Act 2, Scene 4)

Quick quiz answers

8 because he has dreamed of money bags (Act 2, Scene 5)

9 because he 'would have him help to waste / His borrowed purse' (Act 2, Scene 5)

10 because of his colour, or 'complexion' (Act 2, Scene 1)

Quick quiz 3
Uncover the plot

On the Rialto, <u>Antonio's</u> ship is reported wrecked: Shylock hears the 'good news' from <u>Tubal</u> and resolves to <u>'have the heart of him'</u>. In Belmont, Bassanio chooses the <u>lead</u> casket, and wins Portia — while <u>Gratiano</u> declares his love for Nerissa. Salerio appears with a letter from Antonio. Portia offers to pay <u>36,000 ducats</u> to cancel Antonio's bond and sends Bassanio to his friend — meanwhile planning to <u>go disguised to Venice</u>. In Venice, Antonio resigns himself to death, if he can only <u>see Bassanio once more</u>. Left in Belmont, Jessica and <u>Lorenzo</u> start their life together.

Who? What? Where? When? Why?

1 Bassanio and Gratiano; Portia and Nerissa (Act 3, Scene 2)

2 Lorenzo and Jessica (Act 3, Scene 4)

3 Antonio (Act 3, Scene 2)

4 house, servants and self (Act 3, Scene 2)

5 Shylock's flesh and Jessica's (Act 3, Scene 1)

6 the treasure 'stolen' by his daughter, plus more money 'spent in the search' for them (Act 3, Scene 1)

7 at a monastery two miles away from Portia's house in Belmont (Act 3, Scene 4)

8 Doctor Bellario; Padua; 'notes and garments' (Act 3, Scene 4)

9 because she is afraid Bassanio will fail (Act 3, Scene 2)

10 because he has 'deliver'd' many debtors from Shylock's clutches (Act 3, Scene 3)

Quick quiz 4
Uncover the plot

1 Before the court, Shylock is adamant in his demand for <u>the pound of flesh</u>. <u>Bassanio</u> tries to encourage Antonio. Portia appears as the lawyer <u>Balthasar</u> and, after an appeal for <u>mercy</u>, judges that the law is on <u>Shylock's</u> side: the bond must be fulfilled. But there is a catch: since it is not in the bond, Shylock cannot <u>shed blood</u>. The penalty would be <u>his land and goods</u>. Bound by the justice he has demanded, Shylock offers to take <u>9,000 ducats</u>, but — charged with <u>attempted murder of a Venetian</u> — he escapes with his life only through the mercy of <u>the Duke</u>. Portia persuades Bassanio to give her his <u>ring</u> in thanks. The friends all depart for <u>Belmont</u>.

Who? What? Where? When? Why?

1 Portia/Balthasar (Act 4, Scene 1)
2 have a surgeon present to stop Antonio bleeding to death (Act 4, Scene 1)
3 half his goods to the intended victim, half to the state, and the offender's life at the Duke's mercy (Act 4, Scene 1)
4 half his goods to be held in trust by Antonio for Lorenzo; a deed or 'will' making Lorenzo and Jessica his heirs; conversion to Christianity (Act 4, Scene 1)
5 3,000 ducats, 'love and service', a 'token'; satisfaction, Antonio's gloves and Bassanio's ring (Act 4, Scene 1)
6 by the Sabbath (Act 4, Scene 1)
7 when 'justice seasons mercy' (Act 4, Scene 1)
8 because it blesses the giver as well as the receiver (Act 4, Scene 1)
9 because by compromising Venice's law, dangerous precedents will be set for the future (Act 4, Scene 1)
10 because it makes him Shylock's heir (Act 4, Scene 2)

Quick quiz 5

Uncover the plot

In Belmont, Lorenzo and <u>Jessica</u> spend the night talking, when <u>Stephano</u> enters to announce Portia's return, and Launcelot to announce <u>Bassanio's</u>. In a brief interlude, Lorenzo talks of the 'sweet power' of <u>music</u>. <u>Nerissa</u> starts a mock argument with Gratiano about <u>his missing ring</u>. Bassanio is drawn in, until Antonio backs him up again — this time with his <u>soul</u>. Portia reveals herself as <u>the doctor</u>, and with more good news for Lorenzo and <u>Antonio</u>, the play ends.

Who? What? Where? When? Why?

1 to the doctor of law; for Antonio; for payment for saving Antonio
2 the clerk; it was really Nerissa, not a boy at all!
3 'Soft stillness and the night'
4 in Portia's garden
5 because it is on his account that the rings were given to the 'lawyer' and 'clerk'

Who said that?

1 Lorenzo
2 Antonio, to Portia, because she has given him the news that his ships have reached harbour safely
3 Portia; because she is very well aware that she herself is wearing the ring at the time

Open quotes

1 'The man that hath no music in himself / Is fit for treasons, strategems, and spoils.'
2 'I dare be bound again. / My soul upon the forfeit, that your lord / Will never more break faith advisedly.'
3 'How far that little candle throws his beams! / So shines a good deed in a naughty world.'

Page 16, Shakespeare, © Robert Harding World Imagery/
Robert Harding Picture Library/Alamy.Com
Page 19, Scene, © Kelly-Mooney Photography/Corbis

First published 1994
Revised edition 2004

Letts Educational
Chiswick Centre
414 Chiswick High Road
London W4 5TF
Tel: 020 8996 3333

Text © John Mahoney and Stewart Martin 1994
2004 edition revised by Andrea Stowe

Cover and text design by Hardlines Ltd., Charlbury, Oxfordshire.

Typeset by Letterpart Ltd., Reigate, Surrey.

Graphic illustration by Beehive Illustration, Cirencester, Gloucestershire.

Commissioned by Cassandra Birmingham

Editorial project management by Vicky Butt

Printed in Italy.

Design and illustration © Letts Educational Ltd

British Library Cataloguing in Publication Data. A CIP record of this book is
available from the British Library.

ISBN 1 84315 319 X

Letts Educational is a division of Granada Learning, part of Granada plc.